ECCLESIAL REFORM
AND DEFORM MOVEMENTS
in the
South African Context

EDITORS
Ernst M. Conradie
&
Miranda Pillay

SERIES EDITOR
Renier Koegelenberg

SUN PRESS

EFSA
SERIES | ECUMENICAL AND
DEVELOPMENT PERSPECTIVES

Ecclesial Reform and Deform Movements in the South African Context

Published by SUN MeDIA Stellenbosch under the SUN PRESS imprint.

Copyright © 2015 EFSA and authors

First edition 2015

ISBN 978-1-920689-76-6 (print)
ISBN 978-1-920689-77-3 (epub)

Set in 10.5/13 Palatino Linotype
Typesetting and conversion: SUN MeDIA Stellenbosch

SUN PRESS is an imprint of SUN MeDIA Stellenbosch. Academic, professional and reference works are published under this imprint in print and electronic format. This publication may be ordered directly from www.sun-e-shop.co.za.

Produced by SUN MeDIA Stellenbosch.

www.africansunmedia.co.za
www.sun-e-shop.co.za

Ecumenical Foundation of Southern Africa (EFSA)

Executive Chairperson, Prof. H. Russel Botman
Executive Director, Dr Renier A. Koegelenberg
Postal address: P.O. Box 3103, Matieland, Stellenbosch, 7602, South Africa
Physical address: 24-26 Longifolia Street, Paradyskloof, Stellenbosch

Office of the Executive Director
Phone: +27 (0)21 880-1734
Fax: +27 (0)21 880-1735
Fax: +27 (0)86 768-4121
Mobile: +27 (0)83 625-1047
E-mail: efsa@cddc.co.za
Websites: http://www.efsa-institute.org.za
http://www.nrasd.org.za

ACKNOWLEDGEMENTS

EFSA gratefully acknowledges the following institutions for their support of this publication:

- Die Evangelische Kirche in Deutschland (EKD)
- Brot für die Welt
- University of the Western Cape, Department of Religion and Theology

EFSA

INSTITUTE FOR THEOLOGICAL & INTERDISCIPLINARY RESEARCH

Ecumenical Foundation of Southern Africa (EFSA)

The EFSA Institute, founded in 1990, is an independent ecumenical institute that functions as a division of the non-profitable "Cape Development and Dialogue Centre Trust" (CDDC). Trustees include Dr Welile Mazamisa, Archbishop Dr Thabo Makgoba, Dr André van Niekerk, Prof. Russel Botman and Dr Renier Koegelenberg. It consists of a unique network of participating institutions: representatives of the Faculties of Theology and the Departments of Religious Studies of the Universities in the Western Cape are represented on the Board and Executive of the EFSA Institute.

Generally speaking, the EFSA Institute attempts to promote consensus between different sectors, interest groups and stakeholders on the challenges and problems facing our society. It strives to play a facilitating role by providing a platform for public debate, even of controversial issues.

Both in its structure and function there is a dialectic tension between an academic (research-based) approach and the need to address specific needs of the church and other religious communities. This tension is embedded in the main issues facing the churches in our society. In a general sense the EFSA Institute tries to focus public attention (and the attention of the church or academic institutions) on specific problems in society.

Currently, the focus is on the following priorities.

Firstly, the *development role of the church* and other religious communities: the eradication of poverty in South Africa; the role of religious networks in community development, in social and welfare services; and the development of community and youth leadership.

Secondly, the *healing and reconciliatory role of the church* and other religious communities: this includes a project on the role of women in the healing of our violent society; the mobilisation of the church and religious communities against crime and violence; and the breaking down of stereotypes (racism) in our society.

Thirdly, the *formation of values in the strengthening of a moral society by the church* and other religious communities: the promotion of moral values such as honesty; support for the weak; respect for life and human rights.

Fourthly, the *development of youth and community leadership*: special courses for the development of leadership skills among our youth have been developed and are presented to support the building of a new society.

It is also significant that the EFSA Institute acts as Secretariat to the National Religious Association for Social Development (NRASD), which is a Principal Recipient of the Global Fund to Fight AIDS, Tuberculosis and Malaria in South Africa. It is also a partner of Johns Hopkins Health and Education in South Africa (JHHESA – a USAID funded programme). It currently serves as the national secretariat of the religious sector – for the South African National Aids Council (SANAC).

These priorities cannot be separated from one another, since many of the complex social issues are interrelated.

Dr Renier A Koegelenberg
Executive Director

CONTENTS

INTRODUCTION

On the dynamism of reform movements

Ernst Conradie and Miranda Pillay

In ecumenical reflections on "ecclesiology and ethics" it is widely recognised that a particular moral vision provides the source of inspiration that is necessary to sustain processes of social transformation amidst the many obstacles thwarting such work. Inversely, a theological vision of the place and role of the church in God's coming reign is only authentic and credible if it inspires and leads to social transformation. However, the tension between ecclesiology and ethics in the ecumenical movement is also undeniable. Often either matters of "Faith and Order" or of "Church and Society" dominate ecumenical agendas.

In order to understand the interface between ecumenical theology and social transformation the Department of Religion and Theology at UWC has been hosting a series of think tanks and public conferences. A list of the themes addressed is provided below. The project will culminate in a conference on "Ecclesiology and Ethics: The state of ecumenical theology in Africa", planned for June 2015.

In the process of reflection on this interface between ecclesiology and ethics, between what the church is and what it does, between a moral vision and social transformation, it is possible to identify especially two important drivers or agents at the forefront of such social transformation. Firstly, the role of faith-based organisations (FBOs) as "dynamos" of social change in the wider context of civil society needs to be recognised, together with that of non-government organisations (NGOs), community-based organisations (CBOs) and other non-profit organisations (NPOs). Such FBOs, in particular, seem to be able to elicit and channel moral energy in order to address specific aspects of social transformation. Ecclesial reform movements may be regarded as closely related drivers of social transformation. There is in fact an interplay at work between social movements and the institutionalisation of such movements. Movements can by themselves easily lose impetus without organisational structure, leadership and some infrastructure. However, this comes at the cost of some necessary organisational bureaucracy. Without the movements within which organisations in civil society are situated, the latter will lose their moral vision and impetus. Without organisational structures such movements may easily wither away.

In order to identify and describe the role of such ecclesial reform movements, it may be helpful to describe some of their characteristics. Consider the points below, for example.

Ecclesial reform movements are all driven by a particular vision. They capture the imagination and elicit considerable public interest. They are movements because they are able to move people. The focus is here on ecclesial movements, albeit that they are influenced by movements elsewhere in society. Not all such movements focus on ecclesial reform and often primarily address societal change.

Such movements are not necessarily constructive. The same movement may well be described by some as reform and by others as deform movements. In some cases both characterisations may well be true. By itself social transformation, typically in societies in transition, is value neutral. In hindsight such transformation may be for the better but it could also be for the worse, despite the so-called "good intentions" of its adherents

In all cases such reform movements call for reflection and explanation not only because they introduce some novelty, but also because they are typically deeply polemical. Such theological reflection thus becomes part of the movement and seeks to sustain the movement, but it does not exist on its own and will be counter-productive when it becomes an aim in itself.

In this contribution we seek to identify, describe and assess such ecclesial reform and/or deform movements in the South African context. To identify and describe these movements may therefore be helpful in order to understand the interface between ecumenical studies and social ethics. In the planning behind this contribution the following ecclesial reform and/or deform movements were identified as significant in the South African context:

- A movement offering prophetic resistance against various forms of political oppression or hegemony;
- A movement towards gender-inclusive ministries within the church;
- A movement seeking to retrieve classic spiritual disciplines;
- A movement promoting the greening of Christian institutions and practices;
- A movement to retrieve the values embedded in a traditional family-based sense of community;
- A movement to emphasise the need for an intellectually plausible understanding of the Christian faith;
- A movement seeking to embody resistance against patriarchal structures and patterns in church and society;
- A movement seeking to appropriate forms of Christian gathering and worship other than through congregational structures;
- A movement seeking to mediate and unlock the richness of God's manifold blessings, especially but not only amongst the urban poor;
- Christian participation in a movement to promote the exercising of responsible citizenship;
- Christian participation in a movement to resist strategies of exclusion and of stigmatisation, and to ensure equal access to medical and other services by any marginalised group.

On this basis a think tank was hosted on 28 February March 2014, when speakers offered short papers on almost all of these ecclesial movements. All speakers were subsequently invited to rework their contributions in the form of short essays for publication. Understandably, not all of them managed to do so. Only a selection of these short papers could eventually be included in this volume.

A few further comments in this regard are important.

All of these movements are indeed at the forefront of current changes in church and society. We deliberately did not distinguish between reform and deform movements, as elements of both may be present in each movement. The contributions included here reflect this variety. These movements do not necessarily focus on ecclesial reform; they include ecclesial movements focusing on social reform. We wanted to capture the core intuition of the movement as such without linking it immediately with any particular organisation.

Together these essays provide an interesting medley not only of current ecclesial reform but also deform movements in the South African context. Of course, one could also have identified other ecclesial reform and deform movements. One example is the movement to promote "unashamedly ethical" business practices amongst Christians and others. At the time the think tank was planned and hosted (February 2014) the so-called AHA movement had not yet emerged. This movement seeks to promote Authentic Hopeful Action to address poverty, unemployment and inequality in South Africa. It was launched on 2 December 2014 at the University of the Western Cape, together with the launch of the Desmond Tutu Centre for Spirituality and Society. The secretariat for this movement is provided by Kairos Southern Africa (see the contribution by Edwin Arrison in this volume). Several of the authors in this volume are deeply involved in this movement. If the think tank would have been held in 2015 a chapter in this regard would undoubtedly have been included in this volume. Perhaps this merely indicates the dynamic character of movements in that new initiatives constantly emerge while others tend to dissipate. The story of the AHA movement will need to be told later – probably only after 2030 – if its own vision comes to fruition, namely to organise provincial and national indabas to address poverty, unemployment and inequality in South Africa up to 2030.

Ernst Conradie *is Senior Professor in the Department of Religion and Theology at the University of the Western Cape, where he teaches Systematic Theology and Ethics.*

Miranda Pillay *is Senior Lecturer in the Department of Religion and Theology at the University of the Western Cape, where she teaches New Testament Studies and Ethics.*

1

REFORMED OR DEFORMED?

The orientation and role of Kairos Southern Africa

Edwin Arrison

Introduction

For almost the whole of the last twenty years some theologians and church activists in South Africa have been struggling with the question about what shape the prophetic role of the church could or should take in a democratic society. Different words have been used to describe this such as "critical solidarity", "critical engagement" and "speaking truth to power".

But somehow none of these terms fully captured the imagination of church activists and theologians to energise the church to be prophetic or live a prophetic life. After all, some were asking: Who should the church be in solidarity with? Should we be in solidarity with those who are in political office, or with the poorest of the poor who are experiencing new forms of exclusion? Who should the church primarily be engaging with? Who do we think holds the power when we speak about speaking truth to power? Do the people not hold the power, and should we not be speaking truth to the people. One may even say that speaking truth in a time of deception is the most revolutionary thing to do. I would add that working against amnesia and deception is one of the most important things to do at this time.

This is also Kairos Southern Africa's orientation. One of its most important tasks has been to address the South African church and society (while also addressing the ANC as the ruling party) and recalling the history of the church and the ANC in South Africa and in the process helping to reclaim that history.[1]

After Kairos SA met with members of the ANC leadership in early 2012 to discuss a document entitled "Kairos SA Word to the ANC ... in these times", Denise Ackermann, who was part of that first meeting, coined the expression that we should "engage, but not be embedded". This has been the orientation of Kairos SA ever since in terms of engaging with those who hold official political and economic power in society. Kairos SA was one of the key drafters of a document entitled "The church speaks ... for such a time as this"[2] – which is regarded by some as more "radical" than the "Word to the ANC".

The preface to the Kairos SA constitution says that: "Kairos Southern Africa recognises the interrelatedness and interdependence of the struggles of the peoples of Southern Africa, and the role that faith has played and continues to play in the humanisation or dehumanisation processes in our different countries and regions. The South African Kairos document of 1985 recognises that Church and State Theologies, while often dominant, need the corrective of Prophetic Theology in order for faith to be credible. The Zimbabwe Kairos document of 1988 builds upon this prophetic tradition. This organisation and network is now conceived and established to reconnect and nurture the prophetic voice that recognises God's face in the face of the poor and most marginalised people in Southern Africa."[3]

In the founding documents of Kairos SA its vision is expressed in terms of "a humanity with a kairos consciousness". Its fundamental perspectives and values are articulated in the following way:

- Liberation is an event; justice is a process;
- Apartheid and colonialism should not be allowed to continue "under new management";

---

1   See http://kairossouthernafrica.wordpress.com/2012/08/01/kairos-logo/ (accessed 5 September 2014).

2   See http://www.sacc.org.za/content/SACC%202012%20DOCS/DEC%202012/ The%20church%20speaks%20_Final%20%2030%2011%202012.pdf (accessed 5 September 2014).

3   See http://kairossouthernafrica.wordpress.com/about (accessed 5 September 2014).

- God sides with, and God's voice is mainly to be heard amongst, the poor and oppressed, the marginalised and powerless;
- Empire and patriarchy expressed as the quest for power over and domination of others expresses the opposite of the reign of God; communion and ubuntu are the true signs of God's reign.

In order to explain what is meant by "kairos consciousness", Dr Allan Boesak was asked to write a paper to explain this in his own words. He said that many of those who participate in the movement offering prophetic resistance against various forms of political oppression or hegemony come from the black consciousness movement. Boesak added that he remembered Beyers Naudé speaking about the need for a "white consciousness movement" that could unite with those in the black consciousness movement. But what then is a "kairos consciousness"? Boesak defines it in terms of a moment of truth and then says (quoted verbatim):

- A kairos consciousness is a consciousness awake and open to the discovering of, and responding to, the decisiveness and uniqueness of that moment;
- A kairos consciousness knows that the discovery of that moment of truth is not a moment of triumphalist gloating, confirming our own spiritual superiority, but rather of profound and humble joy for the gift of discernment. We are not the truth: the truth has found, recovered and reclaimed us. We are not the light: the light illumines and leads us. We are not *the* voice: we speak and act because we heard the Voice that calls us to do justice, to love mercy and to walk humbly with our God;
- The voice that we hear does not come mystically from heaven, even though we know and confess that a kairos consciousness is a gift of the Spirit of God. The voice we hear and respond to is the voice of the voiceless, the poor and oppressed, those who are the faces at the bottom of the well. It is the voice of those whose dignity, humanity and lives are threatened on a daily basis. A kairos consciousness knows that the assault upon the lives of the weak and powerless is an assault upon the dignity and worthiness of God;
- The voice we hear is the voice of the victims of injustice, but that is precisely the voice of God. As ones whose consciousness has been touched by the spirit of God, we say: *vox victimarum vox Dei*: the cries of the victims are the cries of God. I have learnt this from my spiritual ancestor, the reformer John Calvin.[4]

---

4   See http://kairossouthernafrica.wordpress.com/kairos-consciousness/ (accessed 5 September 2014).

Kairos Southern Africa and ecclesiology

One of the things that bothers some church people about the kairos movement is its understanding of the church. This perception is unfortunately based on a lack of a nuanced understanding of the 1985 *Kairos Document*'s critique of "church theology".

In a paper entitled "On not abandoning church theology"[5] Steve de Gruchy compares the ecclesiologies of the *Kairos Document* and the *Confession of Belhar*. He finds the ecclesiology of the 1985 Kairos Document to be actually quite conservative. It is not one that is critical of the existence of the church, but one that is critical of the practice of church theology and state theology, and of how the church spends its considerable resources. In other words, the kairos movement is one that moves within the ambit of the church, even though it is critical of the actions (or the lack thereof) of the church. Such criticism is, however, rooted in a deep love for the church.

The role of Kairos Southern Africa

The key role for Kairos SA is to engage in a spirituality of solidarity. Solidarity is often seen as energy-sapping, but a key observation made by Mark Braverman is worth noting. During a visit to South Africa in 2011 he asked several South African theologians: Why are you so concerned about Palestine when you have so many challenges right here? The response he received was that solidarity does not take time or energy away from us; it gives us time and new energy.

It is common knowledge that South Africans are generally better at receiving solidarity than giving it. Kairos SA wishes to change that. For example, the year 2014 is also the 20th Anniversary of the Rwandan massacre – so that it is important that we as South Africans do not again forget about that event this year.

We know that this energy for demonstrating solidarity with victims in other contexts is present in our society and simply has to be harnessed.

---

5   See http://belydenisvanbelhar.co.za/wp-content/uploads/2011/11/ngtt_v48_ n1_a31.pdf (accessed 5 September 2014).

When Christians do not display this energy, there are many others who do and we simply need to link up with that. I have, for example, been at Gaza solidarity events where there were almost no other Christians in sight, just a few thousand Muslim people.

On this basis we in Kairos Southern Africa have expressed our role as continuing the legacy of the 1985 Kairos document. This has many implications, but one key implication is that we constantly engage in social analysis and help guide the church in its responses to what is happening around it.

The recent support of the South African Council of Churches for Israeli apartheid week, an international series of events that seeks to raise awareness about Israel's apartheid policies towards Palestinians (last held from 10 to 16 March 2014 in South Africa), is significant in this regard since a new form of apartheid is being practised in Israel, the West Bank and Gaza. After years of hard work and taking church leaders to Palestine, some of them had the courage to say that they support Israeli apartheid week fully and that they called on congregations to pray for Palestine and Israel. This is an important step taken by such church leaders, but one which they will be challenged both by church people and Zionists.

One pastor in Port Elizabeth, when thanking me after doing a presentation there, says that Kairos SA gives them words that are useful and helpful. For example, we do not only ask people to pray for the peace of Jerusalem, but we also ask them to pray for the joy of Bethlehem. For many people such expressions are quite new. It is our hope that this will give the church the energy to act with sufficient courage when facing various injustices.

Whom we are connected to

Because of the focus on solidarity, Kairos SA is connected with all solidarity movements in South Africa and not only amongst church groups. But we are also connected with global solidarity movements and, of course, Kairos groups globally. Besides Kairos Palestine,[6] there is now also Kairos

---

6   See www.kairospalestine.ps (accessed 5 September 2014).

Swaziland, Kairos Nigeria, Kairos Brazil, Kairos USA,[7] Kairos UK, etc. These groups are growing all the time and will all gather in South Africa in 2015 for the 30th Anniversary of the 1985 Kairos Document.

We believe that contemplation and action, silence and solidarity, belong together. The link with the Centre for Christian Spirituality is important, since it expresses the fundamental teaching of Jesus that love of God and love of neighbour belong together.

Challenges and opportunities

There are many challenges and opportunities that Kairos Southern Africa faces, but let me mention only some. We are more than aware, because of the stand that we have taken, that we are hated by or will be opposed by some, both outside and inside the church. From the outside, certain members of the Jewish Board of Deputies and the SA Zionist Federation have attacked members of Kairos Southern Africa in various ways. But more than that, they are busy working inside various churches, particularly in African Independent Churches, to ensure that a certain narrative about Israel remains dominant. We are not too concerned about that, but we are very concerned that Christian theology and spirituality are constantly being infiltrated and twisted by the worst forms of Christian Zionism. Kairos SA, together with our partners, will do all that can be done to expose this kind of theology. In the terms of this volume, that may well be regarded as a deform movement.

Palestinian Christian Theologians such as Naim Ateek (2008:78-82) and other non-Palestinian theologians such as Stephen Sizer (e.g. 2007) have written extensively about the question of "Christian Zionism". In his book entitled *Fatal Embrace*, Mark Braverman (2011:188) refuses to deal with the extremes of Christian Zionism and focuses more on the way Christian Zionism reveals itself in mainline churches. According to him, a so-called "ecumenical deal" was made between mainline Christian churches and the Zionist community, which entails that Christians should not criticise Israel's actions in Palestine and Israel will not mention Christian complicity or Christian silence during the Nazi period. This "deal" has held over the

---

7   See www.kairosusa.org (accessed 5 September 2014).

years, resulting in more and more of the Palestinians' land being taken away from them. This has "deformed" both Christian and Jewish teachings on God's love and justice.

The opportunity for building a spirituality and theology of solidarity, particularly amongst young adults, is still there and Kairos Southern Africa will continue with this work over the next few years.

References

Ateek, Naim 2008. *A Palestinian Christian Cry for Reconciliation*. Maryknoll: Orbis Books.

Braverman, Mark 2011. *Fatal Embrace: Christians, Jews, and the Search for Peace in the Holy Land*. New York: Beaufort Books.

Sizer, Stephen 2007. *Zion's Christian Soldiers? The Bible, Israel, and the Church*. Nottingham: Inter-Varsity Press.

Rev. Edwin Arrison is an Anglican priest and General Secretary of Kairos Southern Africa.

2

EMBODYING MORE OF CHRIST'S BODY

A movement towards inclusivity regarding sexual orientation and gender identity within the church

Ecclesia de Lange and Laurie Gaum

We should perhaps start by stating a deep-seated suspicion towards discussions containing words like "deform". Especially in church and faith circles, lesbian, gay, bisexual, transgender and intersex (LGBTI) people have been referred to as "deviant" for too long, and this has obviously caused damage and suspicion. But we realise that oversensitivity in this regard could be reason for causing real deform in a movement which seeks to bring forth a more inclusive church and society; a movement seeking to embody more progressive Christian values.

We specifically want to concentrate here on inclusivity regarding sexual orientation and gender identity, while acknowledging that this also forms part of a broader conversation around gender. Sexual orientation and gender identity refer to a rather diverse and seemingly ever-expanding coalition of letters of the alphabet – lesbian, gay, bisexual, transgender, intersex, queer, questioning, a-sexual and allies (LGBTIQA…), to mention a few. This coalition of sexual orientations and gender identities underlines the complexity of human sexuality and gender identity exploding in different directions in recent years as the notions of gender and sexual orientation get further unpacked and expanded. We will refer here mainly to LGBTI people, while we also have affinity for a term such as "queer" referring to everyone outside the hegemony of heteronormative power and wanting to transcend the traditional male-female binary.[1]

A changed and rapidly changing world

We are aware that radical shifts occurred in most societies over the past millennium in which heterosexual marriage was used "to consolidate or transfer property, control social and sexual affiliation, construct political alliances, establish social support networks, determine children's rights and obligations, redistribute resources to dependants, organise intergenerational relations and organise the division of labour by gender" (Coontz 2000:10). Over the past four decades changes have occurred regarding societal perceptions of divorce, cohabitation, being single and having children outside of wedlock. Coontz (2000:12) therefore asks the question whether (heterosexual) marriage has become extinct as a central organising mechanism within society and observes that, "Combined with new reproductive techniques such as sperm-donor and surrogate-motherhood arrangements, the trend (of making heterosexual marriage less central to social and personal life) has frayed the tight link that formerly existed between marriage and child-raising."

Sexual minorities have been part of this evolution and the development of their rights has been intertwined with some of the above-mentioned shifts. In the United States, for example, one can trace the development of gay rights as part of the civil rights movement, including the Stonewall riots (and the subsequent start of Gay Pride) in 1969, responses to the AIDS crisis during the 1980s, and recent advances that have been made as far as same-sex marriage is concerned (Gray 2013:60). Developments in South Africa, although stunted by apartheid, link to the above-mentioned movements.

---

1   We would like to situate our work by aligning it with the principles of queer theory. Queer theory strives to question the normal and to trouble the generally excepted. "While queer studies have become well-known for interrogating the boundaries and categories that structure discourses of sexuality and gender (e.g. the binary distinction between 'heterosexual' and 'homosexual,' 'straight' and 'gay,' 'male' and 'female,' etc.) queer analysis today increasingly brings a critical lens to bear on the intersection of sexual dynamics with other dynamics such as race, class, nation and culture" (Hornsby & Stone 2011:ix).

Such developments found a place in our progressive constitution via the promotion of a human rights culture within the African National Congress.

Although this is not true in all cases, through globalisation and standing on the shoulders of those who have driven these developments, new generations of LGBTI people have reached the point when they can "come out" more easily and with greater confidence.

We identify with above-mentioned developments and deliberately choose to reflect on and bring our LGBTI experience into the experience of our faith, as we believe that these experiences can be reconciled and need to be integrated. LGBTI people mostly follow the process of integrating their sexuality and gender identity with their spirituality and life by coming out outside of their churches. Churches and faith communities have traditionally been seen as conservative spaces, antagonistic towards human sexuality in general, and as non-affirming, therefore not offering "safe spaces" for exploration and sexual and gender identity formation and integration. Their exclusionary policies are often based on the way the Bible is read and interpreted.

The rapid changes within society, however, have not occurred without an awareness of the church as an important site of struggle which continues to assert vast influence. As LGBTI people come into their own with greater ease, they also (re-)enter the religious spaces and faith communities they find themselves in, or even from where they come, wanting to move these spaces towards greater holism in their understanding of human sexuality and spirituality.

Bringing human sexuality to the table

Issues around sexual orientation and gender identity confront the church anew with the subject of human sexuality. This follows in the slipstream of having to come to terms with the impact of HIV/AIDS. Churches have to revisit the way they understand their Scriptures and this leads, we would argue, to more responsible readings and interpretations of texts which are often used in relation to these issues.

It furthermore encourages churches to take a serious look at how inclusive or exclusive their communities really are. This poses challenges for the self-understanding of the church. As part of a movement towards promoting appreciation of diversity regarding sexual orientation and gender identity, assisting individuals to fully integrate their sexuality with their spirituality and building a fully inclusive church on these grounds, our aim is not just to provide more inclusive ministries on the margins of the church for a specific marginalised group, but to also make the point that the reforms needed touch on the essence and identity of the church itself.

This movement towards gender inclusivity seeks to embody what it views as core gospel values (see McMahon 1997). One such value is that of hospitality.[2] We draw on the emphasis found in (among other places) the Confession of Belhar locating God and the church (in the imitation of God) "in solidarity with the destitute, the poor and those who suffer injustice" (1986). The "destitute suffering injustice", we argue, should be newly identified in every given time and context, and they include the alien and the outcast within the church itself. In this present context it refers to LGBTI people in particular.

The case for a more inclusive church as far as sexual orientation and gender identity are concerned also raises the issue of the depth of understanding of God's unconditional grace, love and acceptance. It therefore calls the church to deepen its understanding of God self. Since this movement captures the imagination and elicits considerable public interest and largely plays out in the public sphere, it can be seen as an expression of public theology.

---

2 Vosloo (2003:66) argues for an ethic of hospitality when he states: "The challenge posed by the moral crisis does not merely ask for tolerance and peaceful co-existence or some abstract plea for community, but for an ethos of hospitality. The opposite of cruelty and hostility is not simply freedom from the cruel and hostile relationship, but hospitality. Without an ethos of hospitality it is difficult to envisage a way to challenge economic injustice, racism and xenophobia, lack of communication, the recognition of the rights of another, etc. Hospitality is a prerequisite for a more public life."

What follows is a description of how Inclusive and Affirming Ministries (IAM) as a faith based organisation addresses the problem of homo- and transphobia in the church and to create more inclusive community.

An introduction to IAM

Inclusive and Affirming Ministries (IAM) is a faith-based organisation (FBO) with the mission of assisting faith community leaders and lay people to eradicate the stigmatisation of people living with HIV/AIDS and to build welcoming, inclusive and affirming faith communities where LGBTI members can fully participate in all sectors of their faith tradition. IAM assists church leaders and members to reflect on the integration of sexuality and spirituality, and how to engage with the Bible in a life-affirming way.

IAM believes that patriarchy and religious fundamentalism stand in the way of the full inclusion and freedom of all people in South Africa and Africa. Within these target countries IAM contributes to the democratic process of transformation. IAM changes condemning attitudes by addressing homo-transphobia and negative beliefs/teachings produced by faith communities concerning sexual orientation. The organisation performs the role of a catalyst to accomplish the above. This is achieved through programmes which educate all people on all levels of the faith community as well as LGBTI Parents, Friends and Family (PFF) and organisations; raise awareness of diversity regarding sexual orientation and interpretation of sacred texts; re-examine beliefs and attitudes towards homosexuality and opt for dialogue as the preferred manner of managing diversity in an affirming and inclusive manner. The crux of the organisation's work is to empower change agents with knowledge and skills to engage in the building of welcoming, affirming and inclusive faith communities.

IAM's challenges

IAM has identified two levels of challenges faced by LGBTI people. The first is within faith communities. These communities display ignorance with regards to understanding diversity in sexuality and theological interpretations of sacred texts as a result of fundamentalism,[3] patriarchy[4] and homo-transphobia.[5] IAM refers to this position as one of *closed minds*.[6] Such communities lack exposure to the hurt experienced by LGBTI people in the faith. IAM refers to this position as *closed hearts*. Similarly, there is a lack of safe space for LGBTIs to share their stories and to be themselves. IAM refers to this position as *closed doors*.

Secondly, numerous potential agents of change are disempowered on various levels. To name a few: LGBTI people are often paralysed by internalised homo-transphobia and deep seated self-hate, which in turn disempowers them so that they are unable to speak for themselves and to

---

3   Although the term fundamentalism covers a great diversity and it manifests in a variety of ways, it can be defined as follows (see Deiros 2008:331): "In *lato sensu, fundamentalism* can be defined as 'a tendency, a habit of mind, found within religious communities and paradigmatically embodied in certain representative individuals and movements, which manifests itself as a strategy, or set of strategies, by which beleaguered believers attempt to preserve their distinctive identity as a group'. A *stricto sensu* definition is more difficult or even impossible to compose. Fundamentalism is a worldwide phenomenon. It appears to be advancing steadily in virtually every corner of the world."

4   Denise Ackermann (1993:21) defines patriarchy as follows: "The term 'Patriarchy' denotes the legal, economic and social system that validates and enforces the sovereignty of the male head of the family over its other members … It describes by implication woman's subordination to male figures in her personal, societal and religious experience." She further notes: "What is important is understanding patriarchy as a construct in its systemic nature. It is a societal-political system and societal structure of graded subjugation and oppression."

5   Coleman (1995:134) describes homophobia as "irrational fear or hatred of homosexual people. Homophobia generally refers to 'the dread of being in close quarters with homosexual people'. However, since its inception the term homophobia has been transformed in usage and precision and is now used to refer to a range of affective and behavioral components. These components include a rational fear, hatred, hostility, and/or assault as well as a low grade of discomfort and/or amiable indifference."

6   Closed minds are the result of the refusal (based on ignorance and fear of the unknown) to consider an alternative approach to interpreting sacred text which might lead to a different conclusion; this interpretation of sacred text reinforces the hierarchical system of social organisation whereby men hold the position of power over women which plays out in institutions like the church and family e.g. men marry women and they procreate, there is no alternative to heterosexual relationships; this results in the phobia of LGBTI people that leads to hate speech, discrimination and prejudice."

effectively claim their human rights in a self-sustaining way. This could result in silence, self-condemnation, internalised homo-transphobia and getting stuck in a faith closet. Many LGBTIQ people do not realise that religious fundamentalism in South Africa and Africa (LGBTIQ people in Nigeria and Uganda can end up with lifelong jail sentences) will continue to negatively affect them even though they are no longer part of faith communities. PFFs have no support or sounding board within their faith communities. They become alienated and stand powerless against the hierarchy of the faith community. The growing reactionary activism against faith communities leads many LGBTI's to submerge themselves in the gay subculture which result in further alienation from their families and communities.

IAM's Theory of Change – Called the Wheel of Change

Over the last 19 years IAM has developed a theory of change called the "wheel of change". IAM's theory strives for a way forward in an inclusive and affirming way to create safe spaces for constructive dialogue to take place. It acknowledges diversity and differences regarding sexuality, yet holds togetherness/unity as equally important for the common humanity, all "created in the image of God" and loved by God.

IAM shares its "wheel of change" with allies. This enables participants to fully grasp the process towards achieving inclusion and celebrating diversity. The wheel of change allows the process to be effective on all levels of religious community and the community at large. It is a big challenge and slow process to change negative attitudes and to move people out of their comfort zones, which have been kept in place by religious and cultural structures. IAM staff respond to invitations from inside South Africa as well as other African countries to advance their work in the fields of study indicated. IAM has found it helpful to build strategic alliances within each of the countries they work in. The local people understand the context, law and language. IAM acts as a catalyst to empower these partners to become agents of change in their community. The wheel of change indicates a process which includes the five-pronged approach of diversity awareness, dialogue in safe spaces, empowering people, change agents and finally inclusive and affirming communities. The wheel finds momentum as engagement takes place in the different prongs. What follows is a brief description of each aspect of this approach.

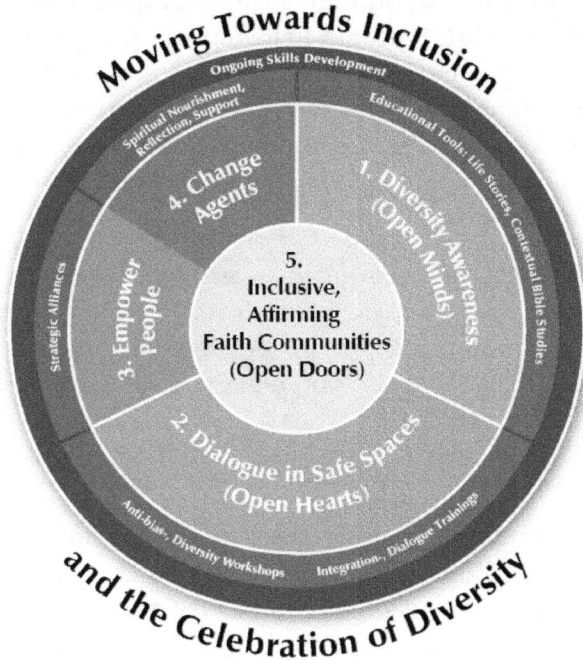

IAM's Wheel of Change

Moving Towards Inclusion
Ongoing Skills Development
Spiritual Nourishment, Reflection, Support
Educational Tools: Life Stories, Contextual Bible Studies
4. Change Agents
1. Diversity Awareness (Open Minds)
Strategic Alliances
3. Empower People
5. Inclusive, Affirming Faith Communities (Open Doors)
2. Dialogue in Safe Spaces (Open Hearts)
Anti-bias, Diversity Workshops
Integration, Dialogue Training
and the Celebration of Diversity

Diversity Awareness (Opening Minds)

Transformation according to the wheel of change starts in creating awareness. The process of creating awareness in faith communities is complex and timely. The lack of knowledge and awareness with regards to the complexity of sexual diversity and the role that the Bible plays in the dominant construction of gender often hampers progress. When LGBTI people share their stories, this yields insight to the experiences, hurt and pain caused by faith communities. This sharing sensitises faith communities to the experiences of LGBTI people. Contextual Bible studies are introduced as an alternative approach to interpret such texts, especially those which have traditionally been used to exclude and oppress LGBTI people. This leads to the next spoke in the wheel of change.

Dialogue in Safe Spaces (Opening Hearts)

Once minds have been opened to the possibility of creating safe spaces, it becomes feasible to introduce the method of dialogue and to listen to the experiences of LGBTIQ people. In this space participants find renewed ways of relating to one another with compassion, appreciation and a deeper understanding of the diverse journeys that people are on with regards to integrating their sexuality and spirituality. This is also the stage where oppressive structures (patriarchy) are identified and where stereotyping and prejudice are exposed.

IAM enables LGBTI, PFF and religious leaders to create safe spaces for dialogue, learning to grow in trust of each other, to grow in understanding of the diverse journeys people are on regarding their sexuality and spirituality, and to find new ways of connecting and forming communities within their faith contexts.

Empower People

This results in identifying key people who can be motivated to make a difference in sharing their experience and knowledge to address prejudice, homophobia, policies and other structures in their faith community structure that uphold the exclusion of LGBTI members. IAM assists and forms strategic alliances with these key individuals to be empowered to become change agents within their own sphere of influence. This territory is embedded in the bureaucracy of patriarchy and heteronormativity which is undergirded by religious beliefs.

Change Agents

The most important asset in fulfilling IAM's vision are change agents. Here we may focus on IAM's staff and leadership. The staff and board members journey with an awareness of vulnerability on a number of levels. They understand the pain of rejection and the effort it takes to integrate their reality with their spirituality. It is therefore not surprising that IAM includes in its year plan a compulsory staff retreat that is scheduled towards the end of each year. Staff members are encouraged to nurture their spirituality as a means of self-care, which leads to renewed energy and vision. It is also important to note that each member of staff has a strong sense of calling to work together towards realising the vision of a fully inclusive, affirming and welcoming faith community.

Over the last couple of years IAM has been purposefully diversifying its staff and at the same time building capacity. This has brought a richness which is appreciated by the team and is hugely beneficial to the work they do and the people they encounter. In some way this emulates what IAM stands for: to be inclusive and celebrate diversity.

Staff members meet once a month for a staff meeting and each member has a one-on-one meeting during the month for support and feedback on their work. It is also important to management that staff members are informed and well read on issues pertaining to LGBTI people and faith communities. Opportunities are given where staff are empowered and trained in relevant issues.

The possibility for deform is always present because of the volume of work and the limited capacity of staff. This could lead to stress and burnout. Working in a multi-denominational, interfaith community context is profoundly challenging. Having to be an alternative voice, continuously, when it comes to interpreting sacred texts, addressing fundamentalism, patriarchy, gender inequality and homophobia can be extremely exhausting and at the same time inspiring. IAM has assisted staff to debrief, during the one-on-one support meetings and in sharing their challenges and celebrations. This support structure provides stability and encouragement to the staff to continue with the journey. IAM has also realised that there is a great possibility for deform as staff may become disillusioned and cynical about institutional religion and the idea of transformation. Staff cannot carry out this task on their own. They are encouraged to surround themselves with change agents in various denominations and similar movements who share the task of transformation and understand the wheel of change. This network becomes an important vehicle not only for support but for further collaboration.

IAM's staff members have progressively built on the leadership of Pieter Oberholzer, its capable founder. Upon his retirement, Judith Kotzé became the new director, signalling a shift from white (Caucasian) male to female leadership. She exercises a team leadership style which encourages staff to own their place in the team and to give the very best of their expertise. The adaptability of leadership in the constant challenging and changing environment, internally and externally, has played a positive role in IAM.

Inclusive and Affirming Communities (Open Doors)

The pursuit of the wheel of change, as discussed above, leads to the opening of doors. These inclusive and affirming communities become the axle on which the wheel of change develops momentum to turn the moral tide. The wheel of change is kept in constant check through monitoring and evaluation strategies.

IAM has learned to work in challenging environments, which can change rapidly or remain stagnant for years. As a movement, it has realised the value of remaining flexible and to be open to learn new skills, to expand its knowledge and influence, to learn from its mistakes and to take care of its staff.

Conclusion – creating real community

Michael Lapsley (2012:35) writes in his autobiography *Redeeming the Past* (albeit in a different context, namely related to disability): "As we who are disabled demand a place in the sun, we are not just asking people to be nice to us; we are saying, 'Actually, you can't be a real community without us'. We don't ask for pity; we ask for justice; and we say, 'Don't just include us in your community. Instead, come, let's create one together.'"

In the same way, LGBTI people are not asking for pity; we are simply asking for justice. We are saying: You are not a real community without us. We are saying: Let us create a new community together!

References

Ackermann, DM 1993. "Liberating the Word: Some Thoughts on Feminist Hermeneutics." *Scriptura,* 44, 1-18.

Coleman, GD 1995. *Homosexuality. Catholic Teaching and Pastoral Practice.* New York: Paulist Press.

Coontz, S 2000. "Marriage: Then and now". *National Forum* 80:3, 10-15.

Deiros, PA 2008. "Fundamentalism". In: Dyrness, WA, Karkkainen, VM & Martinez, JF. *Global Dictionary of Theology,* 331. Paternoster: IVP Academic.

Hornsby, TJ & Stone, K 2011. *Bible Trouble. Queer reading at the Boundaries of Biblical Scholarship.* Atlanta: SBL.

Gray, E 2013. "Edith Windsor – The unlikely activist". *Time Magazine,* 23 December 2013, 58-62.

Lapsley, M 2012. *Redeeming the past: My journey from freedom fighter to healer.* Cape Town: Struik Inspirational.

McMahaon, J 1997. "Queer living: Ethics for ourselves, our societies and our world". In: Stuart, E (ed) *Religion is a Queer Thing,* 125-134. London and Washington: Cassell.

Stuart, E (ed.) 1997. *Religion is a queer thing.* London and Washington: Cassell.

Cloete, GD & Smit, DJ (eds) 1984. *A moment of truth: The confession of the Dutch Reformed Mission Church.* Grand Rapids: WB Eerdmans.

Vosloo, R 2003. "Public Morality and the Need for an Ethos of Hospitality." *Scriptura* 82, 63-71.

Ecclesia de Lange *is a minister of the Methodist Church of Southern Africa (MCSA). She holds an Honour's degree in Theology from the University of South Africa and a Master's degree in Social Science from the University of Cape Town. After announcing to her congregation that she is going to marry her same-sex life partner, Ecclesia was charged, suspended, disciplined and dismissed as a Methodist minister in February 2010. She has been involved with IAM on a part-time basis since 2011 and became a full-time staff member since 2014, managing programme 1 (Transforming Faith Communities in SA) and co-ordinating the process within the Presbyterian and Methodist Church.*

Laurie Gaum *is a Dutch Reformed minister. He started his ministry in a Presbyterian Church in the township of Gugulethu and currently works for the Centre for Christian Spirituality in Cape Town, which focuses on contemplative spirituality and action for social change. He writes and leads workshops on spirituality, gender reconciliation and masculinity/masculinities.*

3

BECOMING MORE REAL

On the fruits of retrieving and practising the classic disciplines

Carel Anthonissen

A personal story

In 1987-1988 I had the privilege of visiting a small community in the northern part of Switzerland in the vicinity of Neuchatel called Grandchamps. It is a community of sisters that, similar to Taizé, was founded during the years of the Second World War and is still today committed not only to a unique form of community and the rules that dictate such a life, but also to the old disciplines of silence, solitude and simplicity.

Although I later returned to the community for longer periods, my first visit in 1987 as part of a Koinonia delegation allowed me to stay over for only one night. One night may sound like a very short if not insignificant period, but it was enough to shake my theological and spiritual foundations.

At the time I had been in the ministry for almost ten years, having been well trained and steeped in the so-called Reformed tradition. But what I experienced in this brief period in Grandchamps was a window onto something totally new if not, for me at least, revolutionary – something which changed my perspective on faith and religion and has remained with me ever since.

After this first experience I was privileged to be able to return to Grandchamps several times during a study period in Germany in 1990-1991. In May 1991 I also attended a five-day Easter retreat in their German-speaking community in Sonnenhof. All these experiences not only helped to further and deepen my interest in the contemplative tradition, they also convinced me that this tradition touches on humanity's deepest needs and longings, which in an ironic way are often so deeply and firmly repressed and buried that people don't even sense or realise them.

With regard to the unique form of contemplative spirituality that characterises the life of the Grandchamps community and that struck and moved me so deeply at the time of my different visits, there are a few traits that stand out.

a)   A tangible spirit of compassion

One incident in this regard will always remain with me. That was when during the evening of my visit I almost casually shared the story of South Africa's apartheid history. Having done this several times before during our two-month Koinonia trip, I now repeated and shared the information in a clinical, if not indifferent way – not really, at that moment, reliving and feeling the sadness of this very tragic period of our history very deeply. But while I was mechanically and unemotionally delivering my little speech, exactly the opposite responses were evoked in the sisters. They were deeply touched, so much so that some of them started to cry – something which took me and my companions by surprise and made us realise how the silence and solitude in which they lived and were steeped every day had awakened in them an amazing if not, for us at least, a shaming sense of compassion and love for all humankind.

b)   A unique sense and expression of community

During our stay at Grandchamps, two renowned pacifists, namely Jean and Hildegard Goss-Meyr – who became famous for their peace work in the Philippines and who also shared the ethos of Grandchamps – enjoyed a brief sabbatical there. Meeting us for the first time, both of them spontaneously put their arms around us and held us tightly as if we were old and dear family. This was an expression of companionship and friendship which I at least had rarely experienced before, but which – this we slowly realised – was also the fruit of a life spent together in the atmosphere of prayerful silence and solitude.

c) A deep appreciation of creativity, art, music and beauty as a core ingredient of spirituality

Coming from a conservative Afrikaans environment where for many years art was viewed with scepticism and disdain, and was in fact seen more as an enemy than as an ally to faith, the way that icons, candles, poetry, music and even the natural environment were appreciated and employed in Grandchamps to enrich the spiritual life was another surprise. Again it became clear how a life lived in silent communion was also fruitful in the development of the aesthetic life, leading to a new appreciation of beauty and simplicity.

d) A surprising knowledge of and connectedness to the social and psychological issues of the day, or put differently, a surprising sense of reality

During my second visit to the community during a study period in Germany, I took the opportunity to discuss some personal struggles and issues with one of the older sisters. She was already in her seventies and, having lived in the isolation of a contemplative community for so long, one hardly expected some profound wisdom or advice, especially on current issues, from her. To my utmost surprise I discovered that she not only fully understood my questions and concerns, but had a deep intuitive understanding of the struggles that modern young people had to deal with. Again it became clear that, apart from the knowledge gained through general education, the silence in which she lived together with her sisters had created in her a deep sense of connection with everything in and around her, offering her insights and wisdom that were not only rare, but real.

e) A committed openness to and involvement with the problems of the world

Although the sisters of Grandchamps live a life of silence and solitude, and thus of relative isolation from the outside world, another surprise was to discover how well informed they were about the issues of the modern world. This happened mostly because they read some newspapers, but more so because they had learnt over the years also to practise the art of hospitality, thus constantly receiving and accommodating a wide variety of visitors, outsiders and volunteers. Flowing from this was a deep commitment to actively serve and help alleviate the pain and anguish of many who suffer and are struggling. For this reason there are numerous sisters working in different countries, usually in some of the poorer areas.

f)   A childlike belief in the power of prayer and more specifically the transformative power of silence

While the sisters remain observant of and committed to addressing the big social issues and challenges that confront our world today, their main mission and core activity throughout have always been to remain watchful by practising contemplative prayer. This ritual is repeated three times a day by the whole community and remains the source for a lifestyle of compassion and social concern.

The prayer life of the community is guarded and sustained by another fundamental discipline, namely silence. Along with the church throughout the ages, the sisters believe that God speaks most clearly to us in silence, while the energy for practising love and forgiveness is also born there. Silence informs and characterises their daily life and activities so that they not only move around in silence, but also enjoy their meals in this way.

After our first meal in Grandchamp, I gently inquired about the secret of the compassionate ethos and manner I sensed in the community. Without giving me a clear and straightforward answer Sister Minke, the leader at the time, simply pointed to our somewhat uncertain, confused and helpless behaviour as we were trying to deal with the silence during the evening meal. Her comment was: "I observed you during the meal and thought to myself: How good to see you like this: uncertain, vulnerable, dependent, even helpless, not really knowing what to do, but eager to learn, because that is the space in which God mostly meets us. And that is where silence usually takes us."

Looking back on that experience today, I realised that in Grandchamp I had been exposed to the fruits of the so-called contemplative tradition with its focus on silence and its gentle appeal to not only debate the God question, but to practise the presence of God – to first of all rest in the Lord and so allow the God of Christ to hold and serve us with God's love and goodness. So that we may become more real, that is more human, earthy, connected and responsible. As with the Carthusians[1] and other similar communities, God is for them not primarily a problem to be solved, or a hypothesis to prove, but a mystery to enter into and to engage with, a loving Presence whose appeal to and claim on our lives reveals meaning and effects radical transformation.

---

1   Different from most of the other orders in the Catholic Church, the Carthusian community, founded by St Bruno of Cologne in the 11th century, has become well known for its total commitment to a life of solitude, prayer and silence. Undergirding the monks' and nuns' commitment to a life in solitude and silence is the firm belief that it is in silence that we experience most intensely the reality of God's unconditional love, forgiveness and acceptance of all people. Here we may experience what it means to live, so to speak, in the lap of God. It is also in silence where the courage to love the other is born. This silence, together with a commitment to simplicity, has remained the basic discipline of all the Carthusian communities over many centuries, and has been called the air the solitary breathes. The Carthusian fathers see it as "the threshold where the soul meets God" (Lockhardt 1985:114).

The Carthusian order is, however, not only a space of personal enlightenment and growth. In a time where people, under the influence of a hedonistic and materialistic culture, have lost their sense and even their need for God, this order is a constant and hopeful reminder that God can be a reality … given that we become silent enough to recognise God among the simple things in life. In the words of St Jerome: "Not in the midst of life's tumult nor in the world of pleasure's round does God show himself, but in the inspiration of nature, grace, light as a breath of fresh air in a still small voice" (see Lockhart 1985:129-130).

In this regard the Carthusian communities serve as lighthouses dotted on our world's coastline, helping humanity to find its way in a world that is often dark, demanding and unfriendly. According to Robin Bruce Lockhardt, who wrote a wonderful little book on the hidden life of these sublime Carthusians entitled *Halfway to heaven*, this is one of the invaluable services they offer to us – "Offering up to God their lives in prayer, so that the rest of humankind may not break its back on the reefs of godlessness" (Lockhardt 1985:107). Perhaps the words from the Carthusian Statutes itself express this best: "By our total surrender, we profess before the world and witness to the ultimate reality of God. Our God-given joy in loving and serving him exclusively proves to the world that his gifts are a reality which can replace most of the so-called necessities of worldly life. It proves that spiritual life is an everyday reality" (Lockhardt 1085:108).

Retrieving the disciplines – affirmative impulses and the way forward

Since returning from Grandchamp, my experience of the value and relevance of the contemplative tradition was affirmed in many ways.

The first was the discovery that the contemplative tradition, with its focus on the classic disciplines, represents one of the oldest and more credible forms of Christianity, starting with the desert fathers, leading into the development of the monastic tradition, with some of its main protagonists the Spanish mystics, and its more modern counterparts in communities such as Taize,[2] Iona,[3] L'Arche,[4]

---

2   The Taizé Community is an ecumenical monastic order in Taizé, Saône-et-Loire, Burgundy, France. It is composed of more than one hundred brothers, from Protestant and Catholic traditions, who originate from about thirty countries across the world. It was founded in 1940 by Brother Roger Schutz, a Protestant. Guidelines for the community's life are contained in *The Rule of Taizé* written by Brother Roger and first published in French in 1954. The community has become one of the world's most important sites of Christian pilgrimage. Over 100,000 young people from around the world make pilgrimages to Taizé each year for prayer, Bible study, sharing and communal work. Through the community's ecumenical outlook, they are encouraged to live in the spirit of kindness, simplicity and reconciliation. See http://en.wikipedia.org/wiki/Taiz%C3%A9_Community (accessed 12 August 2014).

3   The Iona Community, founded in 1938 by the Rev. George MacLeod, is an ecumenical Christian community of men and women from different walks of life and different traditions in the Christian church. Its headquarters are in Glasgow, Scotland, where its publishing house Wild Goose Publications is also based, but its main activities take place on the island of Iona, and to a lesser extent also on Mull, in Argyll and Bute. The community began as a project led by George MacLeod, at that time Church of Scotland minister in Govan, Glasgow, to close the gap which he perceived between the Church and working people. He took a group of ministers and working men to Iona to rebuild the ruined medieval Iona Abbey together. The community which grew out of this was initially under the supervision of an Iona Community Board reporting to the Church of Scotland's General Assembly, but later the formal links with the Church of Scotland were loosened to allow the community more scope for ecumenical involvement. See http://en.wikipedia.org/wiki/Iona (accessed 12 August 2014).

4   L'Arche is an international federation dedicated to the creation and growth of homes, programmes and support networks with people who have intellectual disabilities. It was founded in 1964 when Jean Vanier, the son of Canadian Governor General Georges Vanier and Pauline Vanier, welcomed two men with disabilities into his home in the town of Trosly-Breuil, France. Today, it

Grandchamp,[5] Corry Meela[6] and Shalem.[7]

My study on the credibility of the church in the theology of the German theologian Dietrich Bonhoeffer (see Anthonissen 1993)[8] further convinced me of the ongoing relevance of these disciplines within the context of theological training and especially the church's vocation and struggle to be a sign of hope and transformation in the world – especially in a world

is an international organisation operating 146 communities in 35 countries, and on all five continents. Worldwide, L'Arche is organised into regional and national groupings of independent, locally operated agencies which it calls "communities". Each L'Arche community normally comprises a number of homes and, in many cases, apartments and day programmes as well. Currently, there are 146 L'Arche communities in 35 countries. See http://en.wikipedia.org/wiki/L'Arche (accessed 12 August 2014).

5   In the 1930s a few women in the Reformed Church from French-speaking Switzerland rediscovered the importance of silence in their life of faith. They experienced the Word of God resonating within themselves and bearing fruit in their daily life. They prepared spiritual retreats. at first once a year, in a house at Grandchamp. In the course of time these retreats multiplied to include many others. Such is the nourishing earth in which the Community was born. It was not long before the need was clearly felt to keep the house open throughout the year to provide a continual presence of prayer. Currently there are two communities – the mother community in Areuse, close to Neuchatel, and the other called Sonnenhof in the vicinity of Basel. See http://www.grandchamp.org/ (accessed 12 August 2014).

6   The Corrymeela Community is a Christian community, situated in the north-eastern part of Ireland. The community's objective is the promotion of reconciliation and peace-building through the healing of social, religious and political divisions in Northern Ireland. It runs programmes aimed at establishing a shared society defined by tolerance, where differences are resolved through dialogue in the public sphere and where there is equity, respect for diversity and recognition of interdependence. See http://en.wikipedia.org/wiki/Corrymeela-Community (accessed 12 August 2014).

7   The Shalem Institute for Spiritual Formation is a Christian educational organisation that offers programmes with the stated goal of providing "in-depth support for contemplative living and leadership". The institute was incorporated in 1979 having grown out of a group that began meeting in 1973 in Washington, DC. The institute is an associate member of the Washington Theological Consortium. See http://en.wikipedia.org/wiki/Shalem-Institute-for-Spiritual-Formation (accessed 12 August 2014).

8   After 1935, when Dietrich Bonhoeffer returned from London to act as Director of Training for the Confessing Church in Finkenwalde, he introduced the old disciplines of silence, solitude, fasting and confession as a central part of the theological training (Anthonissen, 73 vv).

caught up in a dehumanising pace and artificial promises, in short: the rage and ruin of modernity.

Finally, my involvement with the Centre for Christian Spirituality, which was established in 1886 as an Anglican Institute for contemplative prayer and living by Francis Cull with the support of the then Archbishop of Cape Town Desmond Tutu, has offered me and many others the opportunity, not only to practise these old disciplines, but also to give them a home in our respective denominations. The Centre, which had since then developed in a full-blown ecumenical community, today raises awareness of the unique power and spiritual benefits of the older disciplines, also of their social relevance, by offering regular retreats, quiet days, contemplative services, spiritual direction, different courses on spiritual formation, and finally, events that help develop and deepen social and personal mindfulness.

The vision of the Centre for Christian Spirituality for the next five years until 2018 as formulated in 2013 reads as follows:

> We see the Centre as a "cluster of centres" – pockets of hope, spaces, communities of consciousness, and of contemplation and action – reaching out across the country guiding people to live deeply contemplative and transformative lives enabling us to transform the world around us;

> We see this "cluster of centres" coordinated from a central hub, from which resources flow and are drawn. The centres and this "hub" are both literal – physical spaces – and metaphorical – a core set of beliefs that hold the centres and our work together;

> We understand this core set of beliefs to be based on an ancient Christian practice – called contemplation – the commitment to and practice of 'the language of silence'. In this daily silence, we are nourished and transformed by God's unconditional love and grow in our discernment of God's calling to us to build a just and inclusive world, and we surrender to that love.

The vision statement then adds "From our centres we see a variety of gifts and offerings emerging." These include the following:

- communities and especially communities of young people immersing themselves in contemplation accompanied and inspired by an African-Taizé-type style of worship;
- people engaged in specially designed liturgies and rituals of contemplation and action that challenge and inspire them;
- people on retreats finding solace and nurture in a hungry and challenging world;
- people experiencing, sharing and learning the art of spiritual direction and discernment;
- people awoken, deepened and transformed through their encounters with our specific programmes, transforming their relationships, places of work, worship and communities;
- people connecting to and engaged with our offerings through our actual and virtual network.

The vision statement continues:

> We also see our centres staffed by full-time professionals and volunteers; well cared for and enabled to develop, market and facilitate the offerings, using technologies that reach out to the centre's diverse members, bringing us together in a community that is both real and virtual;

> Our vision is of our community both virtual and real daily immersing ourselves in the silent, healing and transformational presence of God, and sharing this in acts of compassionate and innovative solidarity with all humankind.

On the basis of this vision the mission statement reads:

> Our mission is to build our cluster or community of centres, to enter daily into the silence, to offer our liturgies, rituals and programmes and with God to engage in the transformation of the world.

One of the more exciting thoughts that is currently being discussed and explored is the possibility of founding a new contemplative order within the context of the Afrikaans community. A few young people are at it this very moment exploring this idea and possibility.

If I must summarise the value of the old disciplines in my life as they were transmitted to me, first by Grandchamps but later also by the Centre for

Christian Spirituality, Taizé in France, Shalem in America and several other organisations and individuals, it will be as follows:

- They have offered me a shorter route to the heart of the gospel than any other tradition I have come across so far, and

- They introduced me to the most difficult experiment which humans can undertake and that is to practise true and honest community.

This experiment in communion, in a life together, with its roots in silence and contemplation – which is the very heart of the gospel and especially the identity and the witness of the church[9] – still needs to be tried and tested more widely and bravely in South Africa.

Bibliography

Anthonissen, C 1993. Die Geloofwaardigheid van die Kerk in die Teologie van Dietrich Bonhoeffer. D.Th. Proefskrif, Universiteit van Stellenbosch.

Brother Roger 1980. *Parable of Community*. London: Mowbray.

Brother Roger 2000. *The Sources of Taizé: No greater Love*. London: Continuum.

Lockhardt, RB 1985. *Halfway to Heaven: The Hidden Life of the Sublime Carthusians*. London: Thames Methuen.

Millar, P 1998. *An Iona Prayer Book*. Norwich: The Canterbury Press.

Rohr, R 1993. *Near Occasions of Grace*. Maryknoll: Orbis Books.

Carel Anthonissen is the Director of the Centre for Christian Spirituality based in Cape Town.

---

9   In his book *Near Occasions of Grace* the Franciscan priest Richard Rohr (1993) shows how the church over centuries narrowed its full vision of peoplehood to an almost total preoccupation with private persons and their devotional needs. In his words: "There is no other form of Christian life except a common one … Until and unless Christ is someone happening between people, the gospel remains largely an abstraction" (Rohr 1993:50).

4

GREENING CHRISTIAN INSTITUTIONS AND PRACTICES

An emerging ecclesial reform movement

Kate Davies

Introduction

Ecotheology and environmental justice activism have been latecomers to the field of contemporary ecclesial movements. With shared values of simplicity and concern for the poor and oppressed, and for justice and equity, it is curious that it has taken religious institutions so long to respond to the global environmental crisis. The sustainable development discourse of the secular world helped the church make the link between social and ecological justice, but an anthropocentric worldview hindered the emergence of a transforming eco-theological agenda in most Christian communities. Very late in the day Christian leadership is now beginning to recognise that planetary sustainability and caring for creation must become an integral part of the ministry of the church.

This contribution records a brief history of the environmental movement and church involvement in ecojustice activism. It makes suggestions as to why Christian churches in South Africa, with a historical involvement in social justice, have not responded sooner to the crisis. A new voice of concern from faith communities is beginning to emerge alongside the confident "green economy" discourse of global institutions and corporations. With the realisation that human behaviour is seriously threatening the delicate balance of life on the planet, the need for a unifying and transforming tipping point to mainstream this emerging ecclesial reform movement is discussed.

Scriptural guidelines

> You make springs gush forth in the valleys; they flow between the hills, giving drink to every wild animal; the wild asses quench their thirst. By the streams the birds of the air have their habitation; they sing among the branches. From your lofty abode you water the mountains; the earth is satisfied with the fruit of your work. (Psalm 104:10-13, NRSV version from the Green Bible 2008)

The Bible is filled with ecological wisdom, but with scales over our eyes we have neglected to read it through a green lens. Scripture has guided and directed human behaviour for over two millennia. At the same time the church has responded to people's lived experiences and social conditions by interpreting and applying scriptural guidance to the social and political mores of the time. Thus ecclesial reform has influenced social movements and vice versa.

In the sixteenth and seventeenth centuries the Church of England's *Book of Common Prayer* readings emphasised humility and obedience to the authorities at a time when it was important to uphold the monarchy and avoid religious conflict. Growing awareness of human rights was expressed in the church-led campaign against slavery. Twentieth-century campaigns for racial, gender, health and other human rights have seen the church draw on scriptural values of justice and equity along with a greater emphasis on love, compassion and mercy. As needs arose and conditions changed, scriptural passages were "discovered", re-interpreted and used to lead and support reform initiatives. "New" liberation theologies emerging first in Latin America in the 1970s reflected the lived experiences of the social and economic conditions of the time. Until recently there has been a notable voice missing from these emerging theologies in the church's struggle for justice. It is the voice of the "other than human" or what Berry (1999) terms the "earth community".

For two thousand years church doctrine and practice have been unapologetically anthropocentric. By being given dominion over the earth, "man" had a scriptural mandate to subdue it (Gen. 1:28). More recent interpretations call on humans to be "stewards" or "custodians" and for God's people to be "earth-keepers" (Gen. 2:15), but these passages still emphasise the superiority and authority of humans over the rest of creation, even though it is nuanced with more caring language.

Modernity: religion alienated from science and economics

Enlightenment thinking in the modern era constructed an epistemology of separation. The rift between science and religion further contributed to the alienation of people from the earth. Using the rational language of science to describe God's creative handiwork as "the environment" has depersonalised the spiritual relationship that indigenous communities have had with the land over eons of human history. Globalisation, the modern religion of consumerism and a belief in the myth that there can be perpetual economic growth on a finite planet, has further eroded these values. Global governance systems now encourage people to view every aspect of nature as "an ecosystem service". Government institutions and corporations espouse the notion that the world can be "saved" from the environmental crisis by "greening" the economy. Many even advocate putting a price on essential life-support systems such as carbon and water (Kaggwa et al. 2013; UNEP 2013).

What is the reality? The human population is now in excess of seven billion. Global food systems and energy and water supplies are insecure. Many of the earth's natural habitats are severely degraded. Climate change is a lived reality, especially amongst vulnerable communities in the so-called developing world and oceanic islands. Thousands of species of indigenous plants and animals are becoming extinct. In the midst of this many people are trapped in a cycle of degrading and often hopeless poverty.

Why has the church been deaf to the cry of the earth when the Scriptures are filled with references of God's love for the whole world, the cosmos (John 3:16)? Why has the church not responded and joined forces with environmental movements when evidence of environmental destruction is all around us? This is puzzling since Christians and environmentalists share many common core values: values of living more simply and sustainably; sharing and caring for the oppressed and disadvantaged neighbour (in this case, the earth community as neighbour); common principles that reject excessive accumulation of wealth that lead to gross inequality. Both sectors have traditions of activism and advocacy for justice.

Where is the ecclesial reform that challenges the salvation myth of the green economy and perpetual economic growth? Why is the prophetic voice of the church, so bold during the anti-apartheid era, not advocating for transformation towards ecojustice when the earth is in crisis? Why the silence when the evidence of environmental collapse is all around us? Why do we not recognise the impact of ecological collapse on human wellbeing?

We are dealing with the legacy of mistrust and separation between science and religion left by so-called "Enlightenment" thinking. Some Christians suspect environmental organisations of "new" age or pagan leanings, while the church has been criticised for discounting rational science. There is, however, a growing call for mainstream religion and science to be in dialogue (Nürnberger 2011). Einstein is reputed to have said: "Science without religion is lame and religion without science is blind". Science has "taken the world apart", but if there is to be behavioural change, the world needs a moral compass that touches people's hearts. Religions may now hold the key for a different vision of the future. This is the transforming ecclesial movement we are concerned with.

Environmental justice movements: where is the church?

For millennia human communities lived close to the earth with an intimate knowledge and understanding of their dependence on nature and her cycles. Permanent settlements and expanding populations gradually grew the human ecological footprint. With the expansion of towns and cities, people began to lose their spiritual connection with the natural world. Emerging Abrahamic faiths set "man" apart from and over nature. "Wilderness" became a place to be feared. In spite of this, Christian ecological wisdom and sensitivity surfaced in various forms over the centuries. The early desert fathers, the Celtic Church, the Benedictines and latterly the Puritans in North America all recognised forms of human-nature connectivity and responsibility. Inspirational individuals such as Hildegard of Bingen, St Francis of Assissi and Meister Eckhart have left us with a wellspring of thoughts and writings about human-nature relationships. Here are the foundations of collective wisdom and a moral compass to link faith with nature (Conradie & Field 2000).

The lack of a Christian response to the current environmental crisis may in part be blamed on the legacy of dualism left us by European philosophers and scientists from the 16th, 17th and 18th centuries. The "age of enlightenment" as it came to be known, deconstructed the world and promoted the separation of body and soul and people and nature. Science and religion spoke different languages and didn't listen to or understand each other.

The industrial revolution opened up wide-ranging "development" opportunities to the human family, but it wrought enormous and irreversible damage on the environment. The struggle for liberation and human rights so dominated the social agenda of the church during the 20th century that it was blind to portents of the earth in distress unless it was related to a human story. An early omen about deteriorating planetary wellbeing came from the landmark publication of *Silent Spring* by biologist Rachel Carson in 1962. Around the world scientists were beginning to pick up signs of a looming environmental crisis. *The Limits to Growth* by the Club of Rome (Meadows et al. 1972) and Schumacher's *Small is Beautiful* (1974) and the 1972 UN Conference on the Human Environment helped the global community begin to make the connection between human development and the environment. At that time the church in South Africa was dealing with the aftermath of the Sharpeville massacre, the escalating crackdown on civil liberties by the National Party Government and the lived reality of apartheid.

The sustainable development discourse, first defined in *Our Common Future* in 1987 and which brought together the "environment" agenda of the developed world and "development" needs of countries in the south, set the stage for global discussions which have unfolded over the past 25 years. The UN has taken the lead by hosting an Environment Conference every decade since 1972 and regular intergovernmental meetings on climate change, biodiversity and desertification, to name a few. The seventh Millennium Development Goal deals with environmental sustainability.

Specialists from the International Union for Conservation of Nature (IUCN) meet regularly to reflect on the health of the planet. We are learning more and more about the state of the environment at global, continental, regional and local levels, and secular consciousness is growing, but we are swimming against the tide. According to the Millennium Ecosystem Assessment (2005), 60% of the earth's ecosystems are seriously degraded. Several billion people are directly dependent for their survival on the environment where they live. At the same time the disparity between rich and poor widens.

Towards the end of the 20th century new communities of concern for the earth and the human family and new narratives were emerging. These were calling for more ethical and responsible relationships between humans and the planet. The Earth Charter initiative was launched in 1992 at the time of the Rio Earth Summit (see www.earthcharter.org). This long-term participatory process was drafted by groups of people, including many faith leaders from around the world. Respectful of religious values, it articulated a set of common principles about our shared responsibility for the earth, including environmental protection, human rights, equitable human development and peace. This was a message that the late African Nobel Peace Laureate, Wangari Maathai, also shared with the world. Another voice was that of the proponents of Gaia, who saw the earth functioning as a single self-regulating living organism.

Where was the moral voice of the global religious community during this time? In 1983 the World Council of Churches initiated an extended JPIC (Justice, Peace and the Integrity of Creation) process. Its starting point was recognition of the ecological wisdom that is housed in local communities and how this should inform Christian praxis. The first global statements about religious teachings and nature, the Assisi Declarations, from five of the world's major religions, were launched at a celebration at Assisi in Italy by the WWF in 1986. In 1992 the Ecumenical Patriarch of the Orthodox Church declared 1 September a pan-Orthodox day of prayer for the environment.

By the 1990s religious scholars, theologians and academic writers were beginning to explore the faith-environment nexus more extensively.

Ecofeminism or ecological feminism challenged classical patriarchal theology by linking the domination of women and of nature (see Ruether 1994, 1996, 2000). Reuther outlines the theological and ethical need to balance justice for the oppressed and sustainability for the earth in order to create flourishing communities (Ruether 2000:10).

Religious concern for nature was opened up to a much wider lay readership in particular by two accessible books *To Care for the Earth* (1986) and *The Greening of the Church* (1990) by Sean McDonagh, a Catholic priest and long-time missionary in the Philippines. McDonagh followed these with other books on the church and extinction, patenting life, water and climate change. Thomas Berry, another Catholic eco-theologian, or "geologian" as he called himself, was also writing books about a "new" earth spirituality that appealed to a wider audience (Berry 1988, 1999; Swimme & Berry 1992). The literature was growing and soon spread to South Africa.

Christians and ecojustice in a democratic South Africa

South Africa acquired a new Constitution in 1996 with environmental rights enshrined in Section 24 of the Bill of Rights. Civil society movements concerned about the state of the environment and ecojustice and not just wildlife and wilderness conservation were emerging in organisations such as Earthlife Africa (1988), the Environmental Justice Network Forum (1992), Timberwatch (1995) and Biowatch (1997). A few academics began to focus their research on people, poverty and the environment (see Wilson & Ramphele 1989; Cock & Koch, 1991; Ramphele & McDowell, 1991; Nürnberger 1999; McDonald 2002).

With a long history of social justice activism, what were the churches saying about the environment in the new democratic South Africa? Christian communities had the potential to play a valuable role in advocating for ecojustice, because religious leaders were often better trusted by grassroots constituencies than their political counterparts and were in a position to offer unique moral guidance. In spite of this, Conradie et al. acknowledge that the church was resistant to the environmental agenda and in 2001 was not (yet) an important ecojustice role player in South Africa (2001:669).

An attempt by Davies to highlight Christian earth-care responsibility in *A Call to Mission* in the Anglican Church in 1985, a time when the country was "on fire", was misunderstood and criticised by social justice activists. One of the earliest conferences on ecotheology in South Africa was hosted at Unisa in 1987 under the title *Are we killing God's earth?* (Vorster 1987), while the South African Missiological Society hosted a conference on "Mission and ecology" in 1991. The annual meeting of the Theological Society of South Africa in 1991 focused on the theme of "Justice, Peace and the Integrity of Creation" (Pietermaritzburg, August 1991). Despite such initiatives it is fair to say that such theological reflections addressed an emerging environmental awareness in scholarly circles but not yet an emerging ecclesial reform movement. Even after the 1994 elections and the achievement of democracy, further attempts to galvanise action by the church in publications like *Save our Future* (Davies, G 1995) and *A year of special days: Readings prayers and resource materials for celebrating eco-justice days* (Davies, K 1996) were not widely recognised. In 1997 the Department of Religious Studies at UCT hosted a summer school on "Theology, the churches and the environmental crisis" – which was apparently not as well attended as similar events on other topics (see Conradie & Field 2000).

The country was exploring its new democracy, struggling to restore human rights and dignity and starting to deal with the escalating social problems associated with the HIV/AIDS pandemic. The challenge of greening the church in South Africa at this time was discussed by Cock (1992, 1994). Conradie et al. (2001) describe a handful of emerging environment projects initiated by a variety of Christian denominations. Amongst these were the environment and development projects in the Anglican Diocese of Umzimvubu (see Warmback 2005), the Faith and Earthkeeping project based at Unisa (see Olivier 2002, also various contributions by Daneel, e.g. 2000), the Mehodist Khanya Programme, and Abalimi Bezekhaya, affiliated with Catholic Welfare and Development. However, barring small pockets of local actions, such as food gardening, rural skills training, recycling and tree planting, the church was not ready for a "new" liberating and overarching theology that might drive an ecclesial ecojustice movement.

In spite of a general apathy, many of the mainline churches were beginning to understand the link between human wellbeing and a healthy environment, and issued statements and adopted resolutions reflecting this. Conradie and Field (2000) list a number of these statements published in the 1990s. Conradie notes that while they may be symbolic in "shaping moral vision", statements and resolutions often have little practical impact (2006:182-183). They were significant, however, because, even if not spoken about, caring for the earth and the earth community particularly as it related to human wellbeing, was now on the agenda of most of the mainline Christian churches in the country.

21st-century developments

A growing level of consciousness about the human impact on the earth's bio-systems emerged in the 21st century. Improving communication technologies that made information more accessible to ordinary people and the screening of *An Inconvenient Truth*, Al Gore's 2006 award-winning documentary on the climate crisis, emphasised what scientists had been predicting for decades. Around the world the Christian church was responding with academic courses, workshops, global conferences and many publications on ecotheology (e.g. Hessel & Reuther 2000; Conradie 2006; www.yale.edu/religionandecology). In South Africa Conradie (e.g. 2006) was making a significant contribution to the local and global ecotheology conversation and literature. Almost every denomination has now developed, adapted or has access to environmental liturgies, Bible studies and programmes providing guiding frameworks for local eco-congregation activities. In 2008 a green-letter edition of the Bible appeared on bookshop shelves. This *Green Bible* highlights "the rich and varied ways the books of the Bible speak directly to how we should think and act as we confront the environmental crisis facing our planet" (2008:15).

From theory to praxis: Slow change in South Africa

Where is this 21st-century ecclesial ecojustice movement being expressed and how is it playing out in South Africa? In 2000 Conradie and Field published *A Rainbow Over the Land*, an accessible and much needed contextual book intended to help local South African Christian communities find ways of responding to the environmental crisis. Although few people know of the book, which is now out of print, it provided a wonderful framework, filled with simple explanations and practical examples and guidelines on how theory has and can be transformed into practical actions. Fourteen years on, it is likely to have quite a different reception. There would now be considerable demand for an updated and expanded version of this useful resource.

In 2002 South Africa hosted the WSSD (World Summit on Sustainable Development) in Sandton, an upmarket suburb of Johannesburg. Members of faith communities participated in the civil society workshops and "side-shows", explored "green" exhibitions and listened to new narratives. They were present but hardly visible in the crowds. The "Johannesburg Declaration on Sustainable Development", a political commitment, emerged from the global meeting, but the conference had little obvious impact on Christian communities in South Africa except perhaps to promote small local recycling and other greening initiatives.

However, change was in the air. In the build-up to the WSSD a group of theologians and Christian leaders worked on and published a powerful discussion document entitled *The Land is Crying for Justice* (2002). It called on Christians to make the connection between social and ecological injustice and to become advocates for change. NECCSA, the Network of Earthkeeping Christian Communities of South Africa, was launched at this time. Committed to stimulating concern for environmental justice amongst Christians in South Africa, the network encouraged "earthkeeping" practices. This was an expression of care for the whole earth community, not just human wellbeing. It also hoped to challenge structures of power and greed that both marginalise the poor and damage environments (see www.neccsa.org.za). While NECCSA is no longer active, it prepared the soil and helped connect individuals and small groups of Christians concerned about the environment. In 2003 the Durban-based Diakonia Council of Churches picked up on the ecojustice theme for their "Social Justice Season" and published a series of Bible studies and liturgies linking faith with the environment (Brittion 2003).

Other national action-based Christian environment initiatives taking root in South Africa at this time were A Rocha, an international evangelical Christian conservation organisation (see www.arocha.org) and the Church Land Project (CLP). In those days the CLP researched and promoted sustainable and ethical use of church-owned land, but it now has a stronger political and justice agenda calling for poverty alleviation and equitable land rights (see www.churchland.org.za).

The Global Anglican Environment Congress (Golliher 2004) hosted in South Africa prior to the WSSD in 2002 led to the formalisation of the CPSA Environment Network in 2003. Their aim was to entrench ecojustice in Anglican Church policy and practice, but in reality only lip service was paid to resolutions and church policy statements. Greening projects, though multiplying, only took off where they were inspired by local eco-champions. In 2001 the SA Catholic Bishop's Conference Justice and Peace Department established an ecojustice desk. Over the years they have organised campaigns on GMOs and nuclear energy (Warmback 2005) and more recently on just energy and fracking in collaboration with SAFCEI (see www.safcei.org). Their current focus is on poverty, land reform, climate, energy and extractive justice (see www.sacbcjusticeandpeace. org). Clusters of local churches undertaking contextual ecojustice actions, many linked to food gardening in support of HIV/AIDS programmes, were beginning to appear in many mainline church congregations, but in no way could this be described as a mainstream movement.

SAFCEI, the Southern African Faith Communities' Environment Institute, was born out of a mandate from participants attending a multi-faith environment conference in 2005. Working alongside the South African Council of Churches and with values based on the Earth Charter principles, SAFCEI was launched by Wangari Maathai at a colourful tree-planting ceremony at Delta Park in Johannesburg in July that year. Because Christianity is the dominant religion in the region, much of SAFCEI's work involves Christian churches.

SAFCEI encourages faith leaders to read sacred texts with "green spectacles" and to mainstream caring for the earth community by developing environmental policies and providing ethical leadership. Church leaders are called upon to set an example and advocate for better environmental and social governance and practices by all sectors of society. Politicians are challenged to "do the right thing" and make ethical decisions that consider the long-term wellbeing of people and the planet over shorter-term financial and political rewards. The SAFCEI eco-congregation programme promotes action and agency in local faith communities, so that they become centres of excellence and transformation that promote life-long informal learning about living more sustainably (see www.safcei.org).

Upping the stakes: Economy and climate change

The reality of economic injustice and climate change, two related global challenges, grew in prominence at the start of the new millennium. Both concerns reinforced the sense of urgency for creating a unifying ecclesial ecological movement.

Economy and ecology: Oikos theology and the olive agenda

Ten years after achieving constitutional democracy in South Africa the legacy of apartheid continued to manifest itself with an ever-widening gap between rich and poor. Around this time a number of theologians were exploring an "eco" or "*oikos*" theology, using as its cornerstone a concept from the Greek word for "household" (e.g. Warmback 2005; Conradie 2006:11-18; De Gruchy 2007a:333-345). The Greek word *oikos* forms the etymological root from which words such as "economy", the rules of the household, and "ecology", the study of how everything in the home is interrelated, are derived. This model provides a theological underpinning that integrates the challenges of social, economic and environmental injustice in the world, our "home". Conradie even suggests that *ecological theology* "offers an avenue to overcome the widespread fragmentation of theological sub-disciplines" (2006:18). These theological ideas might be likened to the secular "sustainable development" discourse that emerged from the UN global conferences in the 1980s.

Recognition that unjust economic systems were at the root of social deprivation and environmental destruction began to be reflected in powerful Christian statements. *The Accra Confession: Covenanting for justice in the economy and the earth* (2004) called on member churches of the World Alliance of Reformed Churches to integrate into their witness and mission a response to the economic and environmental injustices of the global economy. In recognition that economic injustice was creating another *kairos* moment for the church, the Durban-based Diakonia Council of Churches issued a thoughtful challenge to church, state and society in *The Oikos Journey, a reflection on the economic crisis in South Africa* (Diakonia 2006).

De Gruchy wove the *oikos* threads together in his paper on the "Olive Agenda", creating a "metaphorical theology of development" (2007a). Speaking at the SACC Triennial conference in 2007, he stated that "We cannot consider a new future without resolving the tensions between economics and the environment" (De Gruchy 2007b). Using the symbol of the olive branch as a biblical metaphor for peace, he merges into one integrated story the historically conflicting interests of the "brown" poverty agenda and the "green" environmental sustainability agenda, the latter so often interpreted as a privileged or exclusive minority conservation position.

The *Oikos* study group stated that "God's economy is a matter of discipleship" (Diakonia 2006:29). The churches in South Africa were now receiving an unambiguous message about how economic injustice and the growing commodification of the earth had become drivers of human poverty and environmental degradation.

Climate change

The world experienced more intense and unpredictable weather events, droughts, floods and storms in the first decade of the 21st century than at any other time in recorded human history (Coumou & Rahmstorf 2012). International climate talks focused on securing and implementing the Kyoto Protocol. While getting more media coverage, the talks were still going nowhere. Communities on the ground, particularly in rural areas, were already experiencing the impacts of climate change. Faith communities have been slow to engage with its practical realities and struggle to know how to help people build resilience to these risks and vulnerabilities.

Climate change has been on the agenda of the WCC for several decades. Recognising the disconnect between science and political behaviour, the WCC published a statement that expressed solidarity with victims of climate change in 2002. Six years later, at the instigation of the Archbishop of Sweden, Anders Wejryd, The *Uppsala Interfaith Climate Manifesto* was drawn up by a summit of international faith leaders in preparation for the 2009 COP15 climate talks in Copenhagen. The document called for moral leadership, responsibility and hope. The voice of faith leaders around the world was strengthening, but clearly had no influence on the political outcome of the talks.

In 2007 in South Africa another *kairos* process of theological reflection was started, this time under the auspices of the Western Cape branch of the South African Council of Churches. A document entitled *Climate Change – A Challenge to the Churches in South Africa,* issued in 2009, called for prophetic witness and action from Christian leaders and churches (2009). SAFCEI and its partners, along with the SADC-wide *We Have Faith, Act now for climate* justice campaign, began to build momentum towards the 2011 COP 17 Climate talks in Durban. This was done through a series of major conferences for faith leaders in South Africa, Zambia and Kenya, and with a petition calling on world leaders to be honest and put the wellbeing of people and planet before short-term political interests and economic benefits.

Christians and people of faith flocked to Durban from many parts of the sub-continent, some on trains, bicycles and even a caravan of buses from Kenya. While faith communities cannot claim to have had any influence on the formal talks, the hosting of a media-grabbing multi-faith rally in a rugby stadium at the start of the talks and the presence of people of faith, as distinct from civil society movements, throughout the two-week event was unprecedented. SAFCEI was building and strengthening its network across the region and at home, Christians were called on to become more informed, to pray for a fair deal and to lobby leadership to respond ethically to the climate crisis and ecojustice.

While difficult to measure, there is no doubt that Christians are much better informed and engaged with ecojustice issues than they were at the dawn of our democracy. We now hear about and read statements calling for eco-justice at all levels from local church congregations to influential local, regional and international religious leaders. Amongst the newer, influential voices is that of Pope Francis. Addressing a large crowd in Rome earlier this year, he implored Christians to become "Custodians of Creation" and to "Safeguard Creation, because if we destroy Creation, Creation will destroy us! Never forget this!" (Jenkins 2014).

At the local level formal and informal eco-congregations are springing up everywhere (www.earthkeeper.org). A growing number of Christians are discovering and being inspired by ecotheology and many churches are exploring new and creative ways of worship, using liturgies that embrace earth spirituality. In 2013 ACSA, the Anglican Church in Southern Africa, appointed a full-time environment coordinator. With the help of a group of interns, it is initiating environmental activities in Anglican Dioceses and churches in many parts of the Province (www.greenanglicans.org). A third version of the accessible series of worship and activity guides on celebrating a *Season of Creation* (2007, 2012, 2014) has recently been added to the suite of resources available from ACSA and Sunday school earth-care materials are currently being developed (see http://www.greenanglicans. org/resources/liturgical/)

Actions in churches and Christian communities are driven by a raft of social and environmental concerns such as food insecurity, HIV/AIDS, unemployment, poverty, unethical economic practices, escalating water and electricity costs, alarm about the climate, fracking, acid mine drainage, GMOs, waste, nuclear energy and biodiversity loss. Statements and resolutions about ecojustice are coming from the synods of many Christian denominations. At the General Assembly of the Uniting Presbyterian Church of SA (UPCSA) held in July 2014, ecojustice and ecotheology were mentioned in almost all of the reports presented and their *Statement of Faith* now has an entire section devoted to the bio-physical environment. The Anglican Archbishop of Cape Town is to develop a global strategic plan on the environment at an "Eco-Bishops Initiative" that he will host in Cape Town early in 2015 (see Gray 2014).

SAFCEI has a dossier of correspondence from religious leaders to the government calling for investment in renewable energy as an alternative to nuclear and fossil-fuelled energy (see www.safcei.org). Faith leaders were involved in the National Development Plan process and are included as significant civil society stakeholders in parliamentary debates on environmental issues. All over South Africa Christian congregations and organisations are now developing environmental policies, doing energy audits, implementing energy and water-efficiency interventions, recycling waste, planting water-wise gardens, growing vegetables, promoting lower carbon emissions (also with respect to coal stoves), writing letters, challenging the wisdom of fracking and other extractive processes, exploring eco-spirituality and celebrating special environmental days and liturgies.

An ecclesial reform movement: Mainstreaming ecojustice in South African Christian communities

At a recent conference on Religion and the Environment in Africa hosted by the African Association for the Study of Religion at Cape Town University (July 2014), the question was raised whether ecojustice had been mainstreamed by faith communities on the sub-continent. In spite of a growing body of evidence and a collection of wonderful stories of local actions, questions like this can only be answered with hindsight. There are, however, significant reasons why ecotheology has not been embraced more widely by church leaders, while ecological literacy and action have not been mainstreamed in Christian communities.

Anthropocentric attitudes continue to dominate Christian thinking. As long as humans perceive themselves as separate from, and even above, nature and natural laws, and believe that science and technology can be used to manipulate ecosystems without deleterious repercussions, planetary life-support systems will remain under threat. Nürnberger (2011:7) calls for humanity to regain its sanity suggesting that "gratitude has changed to entitlement, needs to wants, contentment to avarice and responsibility to indifference". Deeply entrenched human-centred perceptions will only change when there is a greater understanding of the interconnectedness of all life and a language of gratitude and humility that does not commodify nature as a "resource" intended only for human gratification.

The Christian emphasis on future salvation over stewardship of creation has deepened the disconnection between human and other-than-human communities. Christians need a much stronger incentive to care for the earth than the Biblical stewardship mandate in Genesis 1:28. A creative reaffirmation of the purpose of the incarnation as expressed in the Lord's Prayer, to establish the Kingdom of God on earth rather than to provide an "escape" to heaven, might also help refocus human responsibility to care for the earth and human wellbeing in the here and now.

There is a lapse in time between when greenhouse gases are emitted and when their unpredictable impact is felt through a change in the climate (Hansen 2009). The cause and the effect of environmental challenges are often separated in space and by decades of time. As a result subtle changes in the world around us frequently go unnoticed. The church, in its emerging ecojustice consciousness, needs play a keen role in developing an ethical framework to guide responses to issues of planetary wellbeing and sustainability. These guidelines should be based on the scientific precautionary principle and biblical values of sufficiency, simplicity, love and care of neighbour – the community of life. In a plea to avert an economic-ecological catastrophe, Nürnberger (2011) suggests that science needs "best faith" to be responsible, while faith needs "best science" to be credible. It is time for rational science and creative and transforming hope-filled faith to have a conversation to heal the dualistic rift left us by our "enlightenment" forefathers.

Two of the key factors that precipitate social movement tipping points are the presence of a small number of key, informed and passionate people who hold "social power" (Gladwell 2000:259) with a strong belief that change is possible (Gladwell 2000:258). Eaton makes five reasonable and rational suggestions to advance ecofeminist theology agency: teach radical liberation theologies, support critical thinking amongst religious leadership, become ecologically literate, be active in communities and get involved in inter-religious dialogue on social and ecological issues (Eaton 2000:121). Mobilisation of Christian ecojustice action needs informed leadership. There are champions in our midst, but contemporary theorising in environmental ethics and ecotheology has not yet been mainstreamed into Christian theological training and praxis in South Africa. As a result, one may say that most of the pastors, priests and preachers in churches who hold social power do not "own" the ecojustice message nor are they "empowered" to share and act on it. Teaching and learning about ecotheology and ethics needs to become the norm rather than an optional extra at theological training institutions.

With regard to a belief that change is possible, Ruether (2000:613) suggests that Christian redemptive hope should embrace ecojustice. For this to happen, the interaction between the different traditions of Christian covenantal ethics and sacramental spirituality must be reclaimed. There are urgent ecumenical conversations to be had, because ecojustice is a shared and unifying concern.

Into the future

With the world facing an ecological crisis that cannot be put right by human-scale technological fixes, we need to rediscover spiritual, ecological and indigenous wisdom that helps us to re-establish respect and mutually sustaining relationships with the earth community. This will involve reviewing our theologies and revisiting the scriptural guidelines that brought us to the Anthropocene era. In a world which is being driven by greed and consumerism, and which has lost its moral compass, the human community longs for a powerful, positive and unifying voice of hope. A new visionary ecological consciousness, an "earth spirituality", is what Berry called for as we prepare to enter the relational "ecozoic" era (Swimme & Berry 1992). This inspiring spirituality must surely be based on ecotheology and engaged agency by people of faith. At this tipping point in human history it is becoming crucial that the church provides strong ethical leadership and helps to transform the way we view and live in the world through teaching, worship, celebration and ecojustice praxis. This is the emerging ecclesial reform movement which the world so desperately needs and for which we long.

References

ACSA Environment Group Steering Committee 2007. *Season of Creation 1*. http://www.greenanglicans.org/resources/liturgical/ (accessed 11 August 2014).

ACSA Environment Group Steering Committee 2012. *Season of Creation 2*. http://www.greenanglicans.org/resources/liturgical/ (accessed 11 August 2014).

ACSA Environment Group Steering Committee 2014. *Season of Creation 3*. http://www.greenanglicans.org/resources/liturgical/ (accessed 11 August 2014).

Berry, T 1988. *The dream of the earth*. San Francisco: Sierra Club.

Berry, T 1999. *The Great work: Our way into the future*. New York: Bell Tower Books.

Brittion, S (ed) 2003. *God's gift: The earth, our home*. Durban: Diakonia Council of Churches.

Carson, R 1962. *Silent spring*. city of publication: Houghton Mifflin.

Church of Sweden, 2008. *Uppsala Interfaith Climate Manifesto 2008*. Uppsala: Church of Sweden.

Cock, J 1992. Towards the greening of the church in South Africa: Some problems and possibilities. *Missionalia* 20:3, 174-185.

Cock, J 1994. Christian witness and ecology. *International Review of Mission*. 83:328, 89-92.

Cock, J & Koch, E (eds) 1991. *Going green: People politics and the environment in South Africa*. Cape Town: Oxford University Press.

Conradie, E 2006. *Christianity and ecological theology*. Stellenbosch: Sun Press.

Conradie, E & Field, D 2000. *A rainbow over the land: A South African guide on church and environmental justice*. Cape Town: Western Cape Provincial Council of Churches.

Conradie, E, Majiza, C, Cochrane, J, Sigabi, W, Moloni, V & Field, D 2001. Seeking eco-justice in the South African context. In Hessel, D & Rasmusssen, L (eds): *Earth Habitat: Eco-injustice and the church's response*. 135-158. Minneapolis: Fortress Press.

Coumou, D & Rahmstorf, S 25 March 2012. A decade of weather extremes. http://www.nature.com/natureology (accessed 11 August 2014).

Daneel, ML 2000. Earthkeeping churches at the African grass roots. In Hessel, DT & Ruether, RR (eds): *Christianity and ecology: Seeking the well-being of earth and humans*, 531-552. Cambridge: Harvard University Press.

Davies, G 1995. *Save our Future: A Christian response to the social and environmental threats facing humankind*. Report for the South African Anglican Theological Commission. Scottburgh: Poynter Print.

Davies, K 1996. *A year of special days: Readings, prayers and resources for justice, peace and the environment*. Howick: Share-Net, WESSA.

De Gruchy, S 2007a. An Olive Agenda: First thoughts on a metaphorical theology of development. *Ecumenical Review* 59 2&3, 333- 345.

De Gruchy, S 2007b. Oikos, God and the olive agenda. Address delivered on 17 July to the SACC Triennial National Conference.

Kate Davies

Diakonia Council of Churches 2006. *The Oikos Journey*. http://www.diakonia.org. za/attachments/39_The%20Oikos%20Journey.pdf (accessed 11 August 2014).

Eaton, H 2000. Response to Rosemary Radford Reuther: Ecofeminism and theology – challenges, confrontations and reconstructions. In Hessel, D & Reuther, R (eds): *Christianity and ecology: Seeking the well-being of earth and humans*, 112-124 . Cambridge: Harvard University Press.

Evangelical Lutheran Church in America 2006. *Awakening to God's call to earthkeeping*. www.elca.org/stewardship/teaching (accessed 11 August 2014).

Gladwell, M 2000. *The tipping point: How little things can make a big difference*. London: Abacus.

Goliiher, J (ed) 2004. *Healing God's Creation: The Global Anglican Congress on the Stewardship of Creation*. Harrisburg: Morehouse Publishing.

Gray, K 2014. Eco-bishops' initiative begins to take shape: Episcopal leaders to enter strategic planning process. ACEN (Anglican Communion Environment Network) Digest. See http://acen.anglicancommunion.org/ resources/digest/ acen_march_2014.pdf (accessed 25 August 2014).

Hansen, J 2009. *Storms of my grandchildren: The truth about the coming climate catastrophe and our last chance to save humanity*. London: Bloomsbury Publishing.

Hessel, D & Reuther, R (eds) 2000. *Christianity and ecology: Seeking the well-being of earth and humans*. Cambridge: Harvard University Press.

Jenkins, J 2014. *Pope Francis Makes Biblical Case For Addressing Climate Change: "If We Destroy Creation, Creation Will Destroy Us"*. http://thinkprogress.org/ climate/2014/05/21/3440075/pope-francis-if-we-destroy-creation-creation-will-destroy-us/ (accessed 18 August 2014).

Kaggwa, M, Mutanga, S, Nhamo, G & Simelane, T 2013. South Africa's Green Economy Transition: Implications for reorienting the economy towards a low-carbon growth trajectory. *South African Institute for International affairs. Economic Diplomacy Programme*. Occasional Paper 168.

McDonagh, S 1986. *To care for the earth*. London: Geoffrey Chapman.

McDonagh, S 1990. *The greening of the church*. London: Geoffrey Chapman.

McDonald, D (ed) 2002. *Environmental justice in South Africa*. Cape Town: University of Cape Town Press.

Meadows, DH, Meadows, DL, Randers, J & Behrens, W 1972. *Limits to Growth*. New York: Universe Books.

Millennium Ecosystem Assessment 2005. *Ecosystems and Human Well-being: Synthesis*. Island Press, Washington, DC. http://www.millenniumassessment. org/documents/document.356.aspx.pdf (accessed 18 August 2014).

Nürnberger, K 1999. *Prosperity, poverty and pollution: Managing the approaching crisis*. Pietermaritzburg: Cluster Publications.

Nürnberger, K 2011. *Regaining sanity for the earth: Why science needs best faith to be responsible, why faith needs best science to be credible*. Pietermaritzburg: Cluster Publications.

Olivier, D 2002. The Goldfields Faith and earthkeeping Project. *Bulletin for Contextual Theology in Africa* 8, 2&3, 26-29.

Ramphele, M & McDowell, C (eds) 1991. *Restoring the Land: Environment and change in post-Apartheid South Africa.* London: Panos.

Ruether, R 1994. *Gaia and God: An ecofeminist theology of earth healing.* San Francisco: Harper.

Ruether, R (ed) 1996. *Women healing the earth: Third world women on ecology, feminism and religion.* New York: Maryknoll.

Ruether, R 2000. Ecofeminism: the challenge to theology. In Hessel, D & Reuther, R (eds): *Christianity and ecology: Seeking the well-being of earth and humans,* 97-111. Cambridge: Harvard University Press.

SACC Climate Change Committee 2009. *Climate Change – A Challenge to the Churches in South Africa.* Stellenbosch: SUN Media.

Schumacher, E 1974. *Small is Beautiful.* London: Abacus.

Solidarity with victims of climate change: Reflections on the World Council of Churches" response to climate change. 2002. WCC JPC Updated ecumenical statement. Geneva: WCC.

South African Council of Churches, Climate Change Committee 2009. *Climate Change – A challenge to the churches in South Africa.* Marshalltown: SACC.

Swimme, B & Berry, T 1992. *The Universe Story: from the primordial flaring forth to the ecozoic era – a celebration of the unfolding of the cosmos.* San Francisco: Harper Collins.

World Alliance of Reformed Churches 2004. *The Accra Confession: Covenanting for justice in the economy and the earth.* http://www.oikotree.org/wp-content/uploads/accra-confession.pdf (accessed 18 August 2014).

The Green Bible: NRSV. 2008. New York: Harper Collins.

The land is crying for justice: A discussion document on Christianity and environmental justice in South Africa. 2002. Stellenbosch: Ecumenical Foundation of South Africa.

UNEP 2013. *Green economy scoping study: South African Green economy modelling report (SAGEM).* UNEP and South African Department of Environment Affairs.

Vorster, WS (ed) 1987. *Are we killing God's earth?* Pretoria: University of South Africa.

Warmback, A 2005. *Constructing an oikotheology: The environment, poverty and the church in South Africa.* DPhil Thesis. Pietermaritzberg: University of KwaZulu-Natal.

Wilson, F & Ramphele, M 1989. *Uprooting poverty: The South African challenge.* Cape Town: David Philip.

World Commission on Environment and Development 1987. *Our Common Future.* Oxford: Oxford University Press.

Kate Davies is the eco-congregation coordinator of SAFCEI, the Southern African Faith Communities' Environment Institute.

5

MIGHTY MEN, MIGHTY FAMILIES

A pro-family Christian movement to (re)enforce patriarchal control?

Miranda Pillay

Introduction

"Men will take up their rightful positions in the home as prophets, priests and kings. Reconciliation: marriages, fathers and sons. The spirit of Elijah is coming before the Lord returns again. Read Mal. 4:6" (Angus Buchan, www.joymag.co.za).

"We call on all families to stand up for Jesus, and to (like the families of older times), do His mighty work, all to the glory of His Kingdom. Always remember every country (all over the world) is as strong as their families are!" (Angus Buchan, www.mmcdelmas.co.za).

Angus Buchan is the founder of the Christian men's movement known as the *Mighty Men Conference* (MMC).[1] Having had my suspicions about Buchan's theology raised by Sarojini Nadar in 2009, I was totally taken aback when the 2011 annual MMC was announced during a Sunday service at my

---

1 The following biographical information appears in a number of internet sources and is quoted verbatim: Buchan was originally a Zambian maize and cattle farmer of Scottish descent who started farming in Zambia but was forced to sell everything and move to Greytown, KwaZulu-Natal, South Africa in 1976 due to political unrest in Zambia. In 1980 he started the Shalom Ministries. In 1998 Angus wrote a book about his life, *Faith Like Potatoes*; the book was turned into a film with the same title in 2006. Buchan's *Ordinary People* is a 2012 semi-biographical film that tells the story of the growth of Buchan's ministry from the 1970s to the present, and that of three fictional characters whose lives are changed after attending one of his conferences. (See, for example, http://en.wikipedia.org/wiki/Angus_Buchan; angusbuchan.co.za and http://www.youtube.com/watch?v=SM6SOsekRR0; accessed 8 August 2014).

(Anglican) home parish in Parow, Cape Town. I was more than taken aback when I saw an article in the official gazette of the Diocese of Port Elizabeth, *iindaba* reporting that "many male members of the diocese travelled to Middleburg in the Karoo to attend the Mighty Men Conference".[2] The conference attendee reporting on that event testifies that, "Those of us who went to this meeting must tell of our experiences that took place there and what is happening since, because personal testimonies are powerful, we want to encourage other men to go next year". Moved by the "seriousness" of what Nadar calls "palatable patriarchy", I submitted an article to *iindaba* challenging Buchan's interpretation of Scripture and pointing out the possible dangers of "sanctifying" male headship in contexts of gender-based violence in an AIDS era. My article was never placed.

I work from the premise that MMC is a backlash movement driven by fear of losing power and control in times of change. I will develop this argument by exploring the relationship between feminist movements and pro-family rhetoric. I approach this subject from a theo-ethical perspective using what Iris Marion Young (1990) refers to as five faces of oppression. I will focus on *cultural imperialism* as one of the five faces of oppression. I find Young's view on oppression particularly helpful – especially the notion that oppression is not only a result of the intentions of a tyrant, but that many people continue to suffer oppression because of the everyday practices of well-intentioned members of society. In this sense the causes of oppression are "embedded in unquestioned norms, habits and symbols (Young 1990:41).

Mighty men ... mighty families

The MMC movement has, since the first gathering in 2004 on Buchan's Greytown farm in South Africa, become an annual event drawing tens of thousands of men and it has evolved in at least three ways. It has now become a franchise-style movement in various regions such as MMC Karoo[3] and MMC Bushveld;[4] secondly, the movement has expanded to

2   See http://www.anglicandiocesepe.org.za/iindaba/page.
    php?year=2011&month=6&page=1 (accessed 8 August 2014).

3   See http://www.karoommc.co.za/.

4   See http://www.mmcbosveld.co.za/.

the Mighty Family Conference (MFC), which has become an annual Easter weekend event since 2012;[5] and thirdly MMC has gone international with the UK Christian Vision for Men[6] (CVM) and USA Mighty Men of Valour (MMV).[7]

Some South African scholars have already raised concerns about this popular men's movement. For example, Sarojini Nadar (2009) makes reference to MMC's "palatable patriarchy" and points out how a negative form of masculinity (masculinism) is advanced through a concept of headship embedded in positional power and discursive power.[8] Owino (2012:81-82) argues that MMC could prove to be an "unsafe space" for Christian men who seek "transformative forms of masculinity". Du Pisani (2013:686) describes the founder and leader of MMC as a charismatic revival evangelist who "preaches" that male headship in households is what is needed to solve societal problems. Elsewhere I have suggested that both men and women are attracted to "hope" in what Buchan promises his followers: through their obedience – men to God and women to men – husbands will be affirmed as "men in charge" and wives will be happy because their husbands are fulfilled (Pillay 2011:188). As Jill Buchan puts it:

> The church of God needs men. They need fathers, they need everything *set back in order* because the church is still full of homes that are still struggling with headship and *God says he's going to sort out the church first.* He has to *re-instate the men*, and when he does

5   Buchan says: "The MFC was born out of a vision that God gave me at a conference in Greytown (MMC). I have heard women complain that only Men attend MMC and that they would like to be part of it. The vision I got was to organise a conference for everyone. All families can join us." See www. mmcdelmas.co.za (accessed 8 August 2014). The 2014 MFC theme was "Jesus Weekend".

6   See http://www.cvm.org.uk/events/events_detail.php?eventsID=64 (accessed 8 August 2014).

7   See http://www.menofvalor.com/. Domoka (2009:23-36 not in reference list) points out how "religious principles" could also give positive direction and body to men's movements and cites "Men as Partners" (South Africa), "Men's Forum on Gender" (Zimbabwe) and "The Movement of Men against AIDS" (Kenya) as examples of such movements.

8   Following Stephen Whitehead and Frank Barrett, Nadar explains that positional power and discursive power, evident in MMC, is what may be described as "destructive male power" in a context of violence against women.

that, the women will be very happy (quoted in Nadar 2009:24; cf. Pillay 2011:188).

For many (if not all) of Buchan's followers South Africa's "societal problems" are a result of societal changes after 1994.[9] After its first democratic elections South Africa embarked on a programme to build a non-racist, non-sexist society. Nelson Mandela set the course in his State of the Nation Address at the opening of the first democratically elected parliament:

> It is vitally important that all structures of government, including the President himself, should understand this fully: that freedom cannot be achieved unless women have been emancipated from all forms of oppression. All of us must take this on board, that the objectives of the Reconstruction and Development Programme (RDP) will not have been realised unless we see in visible and practical terms that the condition of the women of our country has radically changed for the better, and that they have been empowered to intervene in all aspects of life as equals with any other member society.[10]

But it is not only in South Africa that change or liberation of the 'other' is seen as a problem that will be solved by men taking their rightful place in society. The Promise Keepers is an example of another men's movement founded in 1990 by retired USA football coach Bill McCartney. Promise four – of the seven promises made by Promise Keepers – relates to a man and his family and states that, "A Promise Keeper is committed to building strong marriages and families through love, protection, and biblical values."[11] No one will argue against the value such a promise holds. It is not that difficult to understand why some wives would welcome the idea of men bearing more responsibility. For example, on the topic of MMC's "empire theology" a woman commented on my Facebook posting saying,

---

9   See   http://www.thinkinghousewife.com/wp/2010/06/white-patriarchy-in-south-africa/ (accessed 8 August 2014). Nadar (2009:25) points to the crisis experienced by Afrikaner men because Afrikaner hegemonic masculinity is being challenged in post-apartheid South Africa.

10 See http://www.sahistory.org.za/article/state-nation-address-president-south-africa-nelson-mandela (accessed 8 August 2014).

11 See http://www.promisekeepers.org/about/pk-board/coach-mccartney (accessed 8 August 2014). Also see www.youtube.com/watch?v=TMekmWiJfb (accessed 8 August 2014).

"let the men attend such conferences so that they can have some idea what God expects from a godly man, husband, father – and not to abuse their roles". For men to become "godly", according to Jill Buchan, "He [God] has to re-instate the men, and when he [God] does that, the women will be very happy" (Nadar 2009: 21; Pillay 2011:188).

As mentioned earlier, MMC has gone international. If one listens to Allen Jackson, a USA pastor (of World Outreach Church) who teamed up with Angus Buchan, it would appear that MMC is the new wave of men's revival.[12] When asked about the difference between MMC and Promise Keepers, Jackson says, "I suppose they would be similar in that both emerge from Christian perspectives, involve music and addressed primarily men". Another common denominator of Christian men's movements is that "marriage breakdown" is seen as the weakness of men to take their rightful (God-ordained) place in society to rule, love and protect their families.[13]

Pro-family rhetoric and feminism

The "headship" theology of movements such as Promise Keepers and MMC is an appeal to men to take charge of their families and their country, while the pro-family rhetoric of these movements appeals to women – who also, according to (re) emerging popular culture, will be happy if they understand that their husbands' are wired (by God) to be "king" (see Pillay 2012).

---

12 See http://www.tennessean.com/article/D4/20131103/LIFESTYLE/311030028/ The-Sunday-Q-Allen-Jackson-Mighty-Men-conference-plans-move-new-venue (accessed 8 August 2014).

13 Elsewhere I have pointed out how American comedian Steve Harvey blames marriage break-ups (or women failing to get married) on a woman's independence and her failure to affirm the man as "head" – as provider and protector (Pillay 2012). There appears to be a (re)emergence of the "Christian" view that the (only) true way of "being a man" is to be on the throne – as prophet, priest and king who protects and provides for his family. While Buchan tells men to get their household ordered as an act of obedience to God, who will bestow prosperity as promised, women are told to behave in a manner that will acknowledge and affirm the man's headship so that he is able to prosper which in turn will ensure her happiness.

While some men and women have from time to time advocated the "reinstatement" of male headship as God's answer to the "family in crises", feminists have continued to expose the patriarchal privilege of men as exploitative of women. Adams notes that over the years family crises have been invoked to combat changing gender arrangements initiated by campaigns for women's rights. She points to the pro-family crusade that emerged in America towards the end of the 19th century and explains that, in response to the rising divorce rate during that time, some conservative clergymen, academics and jurists called for a system of government regulations on marriage:

> As the first wave of the women's rights movement struggled to alter gender arrangements in the home, this countermovement of pro-family reformers attempted to reinforce traditional family norms (Adams 2007:502).

Similarly, in the 1980s a conservative, white, pro-family backlash "blamed" the second wave of feminism for changes to the traditional family as marriage and marital birth rates dropped and birth rates outside of marriage increased. It is particularly interesting that back then it was not only the "threat" to the traditional family that sparked pro-family movements, but also the fact that the racial tensions and the 1960s civil rights movement in the USA resulted in "increasing anxiety for white middle-class men, many of whom saw their economic and familial power dwindling" (Adams 2007:504). Present-day conservative, largely Christian Right, pro-family campaigns and rhetoric dwell on a discourse of "family decline", while it "reinforces traditional gender hierarchy in the home, and demonises feminism for promoting women's individualism and destroying family life" (Adams 2007:503). Current pro-family discourses come from various groups, including religious organisations, "fatherhood promoters, and right-wing think tanks", says Adams (2007:504). Traditional family values proponents such as MMC claim that biblical authority as only they understand it supersedes all other authorities (Good 2006:20).[14] Pro-family movements exhibit

---

14 They usually locate scriptural authority in a specific translation read out of context and with minimal reference to the socio-historical context or linguistic world of the text. Certain texts referring to the mighty leadership of God and godly men, promises of land restitution (return to the land) and submission of wives to their husbands are favoured.

certain discursive themes, including the idealisation of a traditional, heterosexual, male-headed type of family; an implicit reconstitution of traditional gender-based family roles; and a discourse of family decline. Accordingly, they focus on feminists and gays as disrupting the traditional family.

First- second- and third-wave feminist movements are broad generational movements distinguished on the basis of historical situations, goals and strategies. Throughout the historical shifts recorded from the 19th century, one core belief of feminism is the idea of human equality. Third-wave feminism, however, illuminated the racial and class biases of the previous two movements and pointed out the multidimensional nature of women's experiences regarding race, age, ability, sexuality, etc. Therefore the notion of the idealised traditional family as a universal institution is a contentious issue for feminists.[15] Reality and lived experience require one to think rather of "families" as multi-dimensional, fluid and varied. Here an awareness of (and concern with) the way in which context and culture shape knowing is worth mentioning. Gender is a major social, historical and political category that affects the life choices of all women in all communities and cultures (Belenky et al. 1996:4). Social institutions such as the family and the church communicate to women, men and children how womanhood and manhood are defined. Based on a study relating to the experiences of a diverse group of women, Belenky et al. (1986) identify five knowledge perspectives that shape the major ways women (irrespective of class, race or ethnic background) think about themselves, authorities, truth and life options (1996:4-5). These different knowing perspectives may be quoted verbatim:

- Silence – a position of not knowing in which the person feels voiceless, powerless and mindless;
- Received knowing – a position at which knowledge and authority are construed as outside the self and invested in powerful and "knowing others" from whom one is expected to learn;
- Subjective knowing – in which knowing is personal, private and based on intuition and/or feeling states rather than on thought and articulated ideas that are defended with evidence;

---

15 In a (South) African context, the AIDS pandemic has impacted on how families are constituted. So too, of course, has its colonial history of migrant labour.

- Procedural knowing – the position at which techniques and procedures for acquiring, validating and evaluating knowledge claims are developed and honoured; and

- Constructed knowing – the position at which truth is understood to be contextual; knowledge is recognised as tentative, not absolute; and it is understood that the knower is part of (and constructs) the known.

These diverse perspectives on ways of knowing are present in all communities and, I would argue, also extend beyond how women perceive "knowing" to include how other marginalised groups perceive the truth of a prevailing dominant culture. As a South African feminist Christian woman of colour who was a youth in the 1970s and who experienced apartheid as well as the dawn of "democracy", my lenses for "seeing" and knowing have been adjusted over time and include all these perspective at some point of my life-experiences. Thus, aware of the fact that not all women (and men) are in the same space to see the subtleties of oppression, I now turn to *cultural imperialism* as a form of oppression.

Patriarchal normativity and cultural imperialism

As an "elevated norm" patriarchy dominates all other norms and relativises all other power relations in society (Coetzee 2001:300). Thus the elevation of the idea of "rule of the fathers" has developed into a belief system where one social group exercises some form of dominion over another – extending into the political sphere of society.[16] In this sense, patriarchy serves as a "hypernorm" (Coetzee 2001:300).

Young reminds us that oppression does not only mean the "exercising of tyranny by a ruling group" (1990:40). She explains that "oppression" also refers to "the vast and deep injustices people suffer as a consequence of often unconscious assumptions and reactions of well-meaning people in ordinary interactions, media and cultural stereotypes, and structural features of bureaucratic hierarchies and market mechanisms – in short, the normal processes of everyday life" (1990:41). Oppression is often the result of understanding difference in terms of essential natures that determine what group members deserve or what they are capable of (Young 1990:47).

---

16 In apartheid South African society the "legitimacy" of the rule of the fathers in the political sphere was also shaped by its racist policies.

People who defend differentiation of social roles, talents, capabilities, etc. believe (explicitly or implicitly) that a social structure based on sexual differentiation can be justified by "nature" (Nagl-Docekal 2004:2; Holmes1998:106-107).[17] Thus, it is "in women's nature" to be irrational, weak and "in need of", while it is "in men's nature" to be rational, in control and strong in order to provide for and protect "their" women.[18]

The oppressed allow themselves to be conquered when they accept the inferior (often subservient) roles ascribed to them as being "good for them", appropriate and proper. The result is that in the case of patriarchy many women would defend the "system". Furthermore, increasingly powerful religious (and cultural groups) are encouraging the idea that concepts such as gender equality are incompatible with traditional Christian values. This is what MMC is successful in preaching as many men and women are seeking certainty at this point in South Africa's (and world) history. As former South African constitutional judge Albie Sachs laments:

> It is a sad fact that one of the few profoundly non-racial institutions in South Africa is patriarchy. Amongst the multiple chauvinisms which abound in our country, the male version rears itself with special and equal vigour in all communities. Indeed, it is so firmly rooted that it is frequently given a cultural halo and identified with the customs and personality of different communities. Thus, to challenge patriarchy, to dispute the idea that men should be the dominant figures in the family and society, is seen not to be fighting against male privilege but as attempting to destroy African tradition or subvert Afrikaner ideals or undermine civilized and decent British values. Men are exhorted to express their manhood as powerfully as possible. Patriarchy brutalizes men and neutralizes women – across the colour line (Commission on Gender Equality 1998:10).

---

17 For an overview and evaluation of morality based on nature, see Holmes (1998:94-110).

18 The idea that "men are superior to women simply because they are men" is referred to simply as sexism (see Ackermann 2003:30 not in reference list). Ruether explains that "sexism" is understood to be both violence and violation to women's bodily integrity, humanity and capacity to full selfhood – which in itself is a distortion of male humanity (Ruether 1993:242 not in reference list; cf. Pillay 2009b:96 only 2009 in reference list).

Patriarchy is sanctified by both a cultural and a religious halo. As observed in the *Culture, Religion and Gender Handbook*, "Recently, there has been a rise in conservative or fundamentalist religious movements, often associated with conservative nationalism or right-wing politics. These movements are generally opposed to the concept of gender equality."[19] Furthermore, Maluleke observes that many African male theologians who have been dealing with issues of oppression and exclusion in apartheid South Africa are slow in recognising issues of dehumanising, oppression and exclusion operative in patriarchy (2009:31). "African theology", says Maluleke "has remained largely beholden to the supremacist ideas when it comes to gender relations" and "patriarchy speaks to the supremacy of the male" (2009:33; cf. Pillay 2012).

Young (1990) explains that while all oppressed people suffer some inhibition of their ability to develop and exercise their capacities and express their needs, thoughts and feelings, there is no single set of criteria that describes the condition of oppression of all oppressed groups. Furthermore, the contexts in which members of oppressed groups use the term "oppression" to describe their situation has prompted her to consider "oppression" as referring to a family of conditions. To this end she has identified five different categories which she calls the "five faces of oppression" viz. exploitation, marginalisation, powerlessness, cultural imperialism and violence (Young 1990:39-65).[20] While women in different contexts may experience a variety of combinations of all these faces of oppression, for the purpose of this paper, I will focus on cultural imperialism:

> To experience cultural imperialism means to experience how the dominant meanings of society render the particular perspectives of one's own group invisible at the same time as they stereotype one's group and mark it out as the Other (Young 1990:58-59).

---

19 See http://www.ips.org/africa/library/publications/ips_culture_religion_and_genderhandbook.pdf (accessed 8 August 2014). Their attitudes towards gender issues include: a belief that women's proper place is in the home; opposition to reproductive rights; blaming women for the decline in moral values; vilifying women who step outside traditional roles; and active homophobia.

20 For an exposition of how injustice is manifested in violence, marginalisation, powerlessness and exploitation, see Young (1990: 48-65).

The religio-cultural sanctification of patriarchy over the years has earned it hyper-normative status, which gives its advocates access to means of interpretation and communication. As a result, all other practices, values and institutions that have legitimate claims to diverse spheres of competence and existence are subordinated (Coetzee 2001:302). Consequently the assumed superior position given to heterosexual men in a hyper-normative patriarchal society serves to regulate and control human behaviour in all spheres of life. The subservience of women is a cultural product of this hyper-norm.

The injustices caused by dominant patriarchal-hetero-normativity have been raised and challenged by feminists and other liberation theorists alike. Young (1990:59) explains that when the dominant group's claim to universality is challenged, the dominant group "reinforces its position by bringing the other groups under measure of its dominant norms". Thus, the difference of women from men, Muslims from Christians, blacks from whites, and homosexuals from heterosexuals becomes constructed as deviance and inferiority. The culturally dominated group undergoes a paradoxical oppression. On the one hand, oppressed groups are rendered invisible, while on the other hand, they are marked out by stereotypes. In some way or another the stereotype is based on the nature of the imperialised bodies, making their "inferior status" undeniably visible. Accepted as "the natural order of things" these stereotypes are not noticed as contestable:

> Those living under cultural imperialism find themselves defined from the outside, positioned, placed, by a network of dominant meanings they experience as arising from elsewhere ... Consequently, the dominant culture's stereotyped and inferiorized images of the group must be internalised by group members at least to the extent that they are forced to react to behaviour of others influenced by those images (Young 1990:59-60).

South African feminist theologian Louise Kretzschmar gives a succinct overview of how gender oppression operates both as "external oppression" and "internalised" oppression.[21] External oppression manifests itself in

---

21 I have used these categories to explore how HIV-positive individuals experience 'stigma' as oppression. See Pillay (2008:209-217).

two ways: firstly, "exclusion", which makes women invisible and prevents their access to areas of influence such as politics, church leadership[22] and the economy, and aims to restrict women to service in the context of home and family; and secondly, *androcentrism*, which is the "habit of thinking about the world, ourselves, and all that is in the world from the male perspective".[23] Androcentrism drowns or silences women's voices and perceptions (Kretzschmar 1998:173; cf. Pillay 2008:211-212).[24] Internalised oppression, on the other hand "occurs when the oppressed accept or internalise the negative perceptions that those in power have of them. The powerful develop the systems and define the roles that they wish others to play in these systems" (Kretzschmar 1998:173).

Considering the hyper-normative nature of patriarchy, it is not surprising that both men and women find it a plausible social arrangement. Based on selected biblical texts, patriarchal hierarchy is seen as the "order" to which God is calling "His" (sic) people.

Holy family... holy nation?

While the linguistic world of Jesus was dominated by Greek, the Roman Empire was the ruling political force at the time. Ordinary households throughout the empire were influenced by Roman legal and social mores (Good 2006:29). While the word "family" comes from the Latin word *familia*, the term was not used in the sense of the modern "ideal family" of husband, wife and children. The ancient household was a far more inclusive unit which also included people through adoption, slavery and client status. Women had the same physical and legal status as slaves and children in

---

22 For articles where I have dealt with issues of gender injustice in the church, see Pillay (2009a:95-114); Pillay (2009b:219-232 only 2009 in reference list).

23 This sense of always looking at oneself through the eyes of others creates for the oppressed the experience of "double consciousness" as one is defined by both the dominant and subordinate culture (Young 1990:60). The injustice of cultural imperialism is that "the oppressed group's own experience and interpretation of social life finds little expression that touches the dominant culture, while that same culture imposes on the oppressed group its experience and interpretation of social life" (Young 1990:60).

24 Being silent (or silenced) of course does not mean that women (or other marginalised groups) have nothing important to say.

the Roman household. Legally, women, children and slaves were subject to the rule of the paterfamilias (father of the *familia*). Households were at the centre of the mission of the early Christian movement. According to Luke, early believers met in the homes of members of the group.

Let's start with Jesus' family. An extended family constellation emerges in Luke's birth stories, as John the Baptist and Jesus are born at about the same time to women who are related to each other. Both pregnancies are a surprise. While Elizabeth's pregnancy follows the example in Hebrew Scripture of older women (like Sarah) becoming pregnant past their childbearing age, Mary's pregnancy is different. Unlike Elizabeth's pregnancy, marriage is not the means of Mary's pregnancy. While Elizabeth and Zechariah are said to be descendants of priests, Joseph's Davidic lineage is mentioned. As Good observes, "the families into which the children are born typify the respectable family of the Greek-speaking, Roman-dominated, Jewish world of the time" (2006:90). Jesus' parents are presented as devout Jews who attend Passover in Jerusalem with Jesus and other relatives indicating that such public accountability was an intrinsic part of family life. Good (2006:96) points out that "civic responsibility was thought to depend on correct and dutiful religious observance". Perhaps it is because dutiful religious observance converged with serving to maintain peace in the Roman Empire that Jesus challenges and offends the sensibilities of the world. This very sensibility – that the family is the basic unit for religious and civic responsibility – which Jesus challenges in the light of its manipulation by the empire, is claimed to be the essence of God's revelation to the founding leader of MMC.

Luke's reference to households is said to affirm households as units of civic responsibility in Hellenistic cities in the light of the persecution of Christians. This could be the case since, in a suspicious and hostile dominant Roman empire, Christians were seen to be a threat to the religious and political authorities. However, Jesus' words and actions as portrayed in Luke could also serve as a conduit to challenge oppressive social relations.

In Luke Jesus extends kinship beyond mother, brother and sister; the poor are invited to the banquet; the "unclean" are touched and healed; women's agency is recognised. The empire language of mighty men and conquering wars is challenged as the weak and vulnerable take centre stage. It is the "least" and the "small" people and things that count.

Concluding remarks

Under the pretext of its being a "conference" the MMC draws men from all church denominations. As mentioned before, many men from the Anglican Church join the MMC "*saamtrek*" (in solidarity) to learn how to be "godly" men – as God is working through MMC to "re-instate them as the head". This, despite the fact that many prominent (Anglican) church leaders have publicly acknowledged that the "patriarchy of our faith" is "wrong" (Ndungane 2005) and also that feminists "have forced us to confront the patriarchal orientation of much of the biblical texts" (Tutu 2002:7). Thabo Makgoba (2009:3), the current Archbishop of Cape Town, says: "Gender questions, particularly violence against women and children, is of considerable concern, though I hope that with the appointment of a gender action coordinator and liaison bishop for the Province, and an increasing number of gender desks within our Dioceses, the Anglican Church of Southern Africa is becoming more practically engaged in ways that can make a tangible difference."[25]

While the (Anglican) church cannot prohibit its members from participating in MMC or prevent its members from buying into the theology that this movement propagates, it should discern its own culpability in such movements' quest to reinstate patriarchal control. This is important if the church is serious about its acceptance and support of women joining the priesthood. Secondly, the church should offer its members an alternative theology – especially since movements such the MMC undo the strides

---

25 Rev. Cheryl Bird is the first appointed "gender action co-ordinator" and Bishop Raphael Hess is the first appointed liaison bishop for gender in the Anglican Church of Southern Africa – formerly known as the Church of the Province of Southern Africa. It is my opinion that making appointments of this nature is a good structural initiative on provincial level, but that the church (on all levels) has to be purposeful about challenging androcentrism and patriarchy, which are so inherent in its practices of being church. Another point of "intentionality" is that the business of the gender desk (or rather, gender ministry) is an urgent enough matter to warrant the attention of a co-ordinator/ facilitator on a full-time basis and that the agenda for such a ministry should not be dictated by the existing hierarchy of the church – lest it is set up to die a natural death.

made by the church in terms of gender justice issues (especially in the areas relating to discrimination, domination and/or subjugation based on Scripture and tradition).

Observing the socio-historical context of Scripture respects the historical circumstances in which divine disclosure took place. Paying attention to the socio-religio-historical and linguistic contexts of Scripture goes some way toward preventing an interpreter from projecting his or her own mental landscape onto the text.

References

Adams, M 2007. Women's Rights and Wedding Bells: 19th century pro-family rhetoric and (re) enforcement of gender status quo. *Journal of Family Issues* 28:4, 501-528.

Belenky, MMF, Clinchy, BM, Goldberger, NR & Tarule, JM 1986. *Women's Ways of Knowing: The Development of Self, Voice and Mind.* New York: Basic Books, Inc.

Coetzee, D 2001. South African Education and the Ideology of Patriarchy. *South African Journal of Education* 21(4), 300-304.

Commission on Gender Equality, 1998. *Annual Report of the Commission on Gender Equality,* Pretoria: Government Printer.

Du Pisani, K 2013. Verteerbare Patriargie? Angus Buchan, die Mighty Men en Manlikheid. *LitNet Akademies,* 10(2), 685-713.

Good, D. 2006. *Jesus' Family Values.* New York: Church Publishing Incorporated.

Holmes, RL 1998. *Basic Moral Philosophy.* Belmont: Wadsworth.

Kretzschmar, L 1998. Gender, Women and Ethics. In Kretzschmar, L and Hulley, L (eds): *Questions about Life and Morality.* Pretoria: Van Schaik, 169-184.

Makgoba, T 2009. Foreword. In Pillay, M, Nadar, S and Le Bruyns, C (eds): *Ragbag Theologies: Essays in Honour of Denise M Ackermann – a Theologian of Praxis.* Stellenbosch: Sun Press, 1-4.

Maluleke, T 2009. An African Perspective on Patriarchy. In: *The Evil of Patriarchy in Church, Society and Politics.* A Consultation hosted by Inclusive and Affirming Ministries, The University of the Western Cape and The Centre for Christian Spirituality, held at Mont Fleur, Stellenbosch, 5-6 March 2009. Cape Town: IAM, 31-34.

Manda, D 2009. Religions and the Responsibility of Men in Relation to HIV and Gender-Based Violence: An Ethical Call. *Journal of Constructive Theology, (15)*2, 23-40.

Nadar, S 2009. Who is Afraid of the Mighty Men's Conference? – Palatable Patriarchy and Violence Against Women in S.A. In: *The Evil of Patriarchy in Church, Society and Politics*. A Consultation hosted by Inclusive and Affirming Ministries, The University of the Western Cape and The Centre for Christian Spirituality, held at Mont Fleur, Stellenbosch, 5-6 March 2009. Cape Town: IAM, 19-30.

Nagl-Docekal, H 2004. *Feminist Philosophy*. Boulder: Westview Press.

Ndungane, N 2005. *Daily News*, 7 July 2002, 2.

Ndungane, N 2008. God, Gender and the Christian Life. In S Rowland Jones (ed.): *Faith in Action*. Cape Town: Lux Verbi, 301-310.

Owino, K 2012. The Mighty Men Conference as a "Safe Space" for "Born Again" Men to Express Conflicting Masculinities. *Journal of Gender and Religion in Africa*, 18(2), 65-84.

Pillay, M 2011. Church and Environment: On Being Down to Earth in a Consumerist Era. *Scriptura 107*, 184-198.

Pillay, M 2012. Challenging Patriarchal Masculinity in "Act like a lady. Think like a Man: A Feminist theo-ethical Perspective. In Claassens, J & Viljoen, S (eds): *Sacred Selves: Essays on Gender, Religion and Popular Culture*. Cape Town: Griffel, 81-100.

Pillay, M 2008. Challenging stigma in the context of HIV/AIDS: Towards integrating individual and Societal Intervention Strategies. In De Gruchy, S, Koopman, N & Strijbos, S: *From Our Side: Emerging Perspectives on Development and Ethics*. Amsterdam: Rosenberg, 209-222.

Pillay, MN 2003. Church Discourse on HIV/AIDS: A Responsible Response? *Scriptura 82*, 108-121.

Pillay, MN 2009. Women in the Church: Toward Developing Community in the context Of HIV and AIDS. In: Chitando, E. & Hadebe, N. *Compassionate Circles: African Women Theologians Facing HIV*. Geneva: WCC.

Tutu, DM 2002. Foreword. In Balabanski, V & Habel, NC (eds): *The Earth Story in the New Testament*. Cleveland: Pilgrim Press, 7-8.

Young, IM 1990. *Justice and the Politics of Difference*. Princeton: Princeton University Press.

Internet sources

http://en.wikipedia.org/wiki/Angus_Buchan, accessed 7 March 2014.

http://www.angusbuchan.co.za, accessed 7 March 2014.

http://www.youtube.com/watch?v=SM6SOsekRR0), accessed 7 March 2014.

http://www.anglicandiocesepe.org.za/iindaba/page.php?year=2011&month=6&page=1, accessed 7 March 2014.

http://www.karoommc.co.za, accessed 7 March 2014.

http://www.mmcbosveld.co.za, accessed 7 March 2014.

http://www.mmcdelmas.co.za, accessed 7 March 2017.

http://www.cvm.org.uk/events/events_detail.php?eventsID=64, accessed 7 March 2014.

http://www.menofvalor.com/, accessed 7 March 2014.

http://www.promisekeepers.org/about/pk-board/coach-mccartney, accessed 7 March 2014.

www.youtube.com/watch?v=TMekmWiJfb, accessed 7 March 2014.

http://www.tennessean.com/article/D4/20131103/LIFESTYLE/311030028/The-Sunday-Q-Allen-Jackson-Mighty-Men-conference-plans-move-new-venue, accessed 7 March 2014.

http://www.thinkinghousewife.com/wp/2010/06/white-patriarchy-in-south-africa/, accessed 7 March 2014.

http://www.sahistory.org.za/article/state-nation-address-president-south-africa-nelson-mandela, accessed 10 March 2014.

http://www.ips.org/africa/library/publications/ips_culture_religion_and_genderhandbook.pdf, accessed 10 March 2014.

Miranda Pillay *is Senior Lecturer in the Department of Religion and Theology at the University of the Western Cape, where she teaches New Testament Studies and Ethics.*

6

A MOVEMENT EMPHASISING THE NEED FOR AN INTELLECTUALLY PLAUSIBLE UNDERSTANDING OF THE CHRISTIAN FAITH

Julian Müller

Introduction

The God-question is today as relevant as ever and is returning with a new sense of urgency. However, it is about much more than only the God-question. It also touches on many faith-related issues and it changes in different contexts. There are cultural discourses which have an influence on how people and communities construct their faith. The movement towards a more intellectually plausible understanding of the Christian faith should not be seen in isolation. This movement forces Christians and theologians to ask new questions and to enter into new debates about the rationality of the faith. There are two movements, which are seemingly opposing to each other, but existing together as part of a new reality, together with a third movement. Post-theistic ways of understanding God are emerging. It is within this complex and even paradoxical landscape of movements and counter-movements that the conversation about the rationality of faith is taking place.

One day, not long ago, I had to take my car to the garage for a service and was driven back to my work place in the garage courtesy car. There were other passengers with me in the car. When we arrived at the main gate of the University of Pretoria, one of the other passengers engaged in small talk with me and asked what kind of lecturer I was. When I told him that I was in theology, he asked me: "So, how are you doing with the God-problem?"

For a moment I was stunned and tried to come up with a quick answer, but fortunately I had to get out of the car. On my way out I said to him: "We are still working on it ..." And we are still working on it! The God-question today is as relevant as ever.

The God-question

Richard Kearney (2011:1) said:

> The God question is returning today with a new sense of urgency. One hears much talk about the "return of the religious" in contemporary world politics. Debates on the relations of the secular and the sacred are prevalent and arresting. Many speak of a "religious turn" in Continental philosophy or, contrariwise, of an "antireligious turn" in a new wave of critical secularism (Daniel Dennett, Richard Dawkins, Christopher Hitchens). Vital disputes about theism and atheism have not disappeared, as some expected, with the Enlightenment and subsequent declarations of the death of God by Nietzsche, Marx, and Freud. The God question keeps returning again and again, compelling us to ask what we mean when we speak of God.

I assume that this interest in the "God question" is part of the "movement" to which the title of this discussion in ecclesial reform and deform movements refers. But I am also convinced that the movement is about much more that only the God-question.

Cultural discourses

The complex nature of the "movement" becomes more apparent the deeper you go into it. It touches on many faith-related issues and it changes in different contexts. It would probably be closer to the truth to speak of a number of different movements or dynamics that interact with each other. Narratively speaking, there are a number of cultural discourses which have an influence on how people and communities construct their faith in a way that is intellectually plausible for them. These narratives interact with each other – some in contradiction to each other, but at the same time also in support of each other. We can at least identify the following discourses which are all part of a network of movements about rationality and faith:

- The secularisation discourse;
- The growth of charismatic and fundamentalist spirituality;
- The broadening of the natural sciences' paradigm;
- The development of theology away from the revelation towards an interpretation paradigm;
- The unique South African context of disillusionment with the churches that supported apartheid;
- The ongoing and strengthening of intellectual conversations between Western and African spiritualities;
- The fluid boundaries between the mythic and the natural or scientific reality.

In other words: the so-called movement towards a more intellectually plausible understanding of the Christian faith should not be seen in isolation, as something on its own. It is part of a network of narratives connecting with and sometimes disconnecting from each other. It is part of the quest for faith to be reasonable and defendable, a quest which is evident throughout the ages. On the other hand, it is also clear that we are currently moving into new territory and that new questions about an old problem are being asked. Christians of our generation ask different questions and relate in different ways to the community of faith and to Christendom.

Rationally based explanations for faith

The need to provide a rational explanation for faith is not new. We have a long history of apologetics. Christians do want to motivate and defend their choices for God, faith and religion. Such a rational defence was always done in two directions. On the one hand, it is done in communication with an outside and sometimes hostile audience. It is an effort to explain why it makes sense to believe in God and more specifically in the Christian God. On the other hand, it is communication with oneself and the group of insiders. It is also a self-dialogue, a way of explaining the rationality of faith to insiders.

The classic formulation of what theology is in essence probably goes back to Anselm of Canterbury (1033-1109). It says: *Fides quaerens intellectum,* that is, faith seeking understanding.

A new reality

What then is new in this movement? The age we have entered is normally referred to as the era of postmodernism. It includes trends of relativism, secularism and atheism. This new multifaceted context creates new relations and perspectives. It forces Christians and theologians to ask new questions and to enter into new debates about the rationality of the faith. In this complex world we can at least identify two forces, or movements, which are seemingly opposing each other, but which actually exist together as part of a new reality. The first is a movement towards freedom from religion, and the second is the resurgence of religion.

A new worldview with a new perception of reality is growing and it is linked to the liberation of the mind. People, Christians included, are nowadays liberated to think freely, to distance themselves from the doctrinal boundaries of the church, to ask the questions which they were not allowed to ask in earlier times.

In the words of the German philosopher Arnold Gehlen, according to Berger and Zijderveld (2010), people are nowadays empowered to make more foreground choices, while they are less determined by background choices. The so-called background choices are those which are made for us within a certain cultural setting. These are choices you make without thinking, because they are actually made for you by the group you are part of. The foreground choices are the more individual choices that you feel free to make on your own and sometimes against the sentiments of the group. For instance, it is a background choice to wear clothes when you leave your house in the morning. You don't even experience it as a choice – you just do it and comply with the culture. But the colour of the dress or shirt you wear is your own choice and it is not prescribed by the group. That is a foreground choice. This is a simple example just to illustrate the difference. Peter Berger, in accordance with Gehlen, is of the opinion that we are currently moving more and more into a situation of choice-fatigue, because of so many background choices have moved to the foreground. Our parents and grandparents were born into hierarchical and patriarchal societies and choices were made for them. They had very little opportunity to come to individual and independent conclusions.

Previously the choices about religion and church were purely background choices, but now even such fundamental choices have moved to the foreground. People experience much more freedom in making such choices and still manage to belong to the group. Possibilities of differentiating within groups have grown in current times. Traditionally the church had the role of

- explaining the inexplicable in the world;
- controlling society in God's name;
- providing comfort where needed.

In the meantime the institution of the church has been stripped of many of these roles in society. These tasks have been taken over by other institutions and people are making choices without the controlling power of the church. The background power and influence of the church is fading away in many communities. In the words of Grayling (2014:3): "it is that there are other and better sources of these valuable things, which have the additional merit of being far better grounded in reason and more accurate understanding of the world – which is in short to say: are far closer to the truth."

This process is normally referred to as "secularisation". It means that the sacred is replaced by the secular and the church has been moved from the centre to the margins of society. Paradoxically, there is at the same time a different movement – a resurgence of religion and also of organised religion. Harvey Cox (2010) says that:

> Many observers mistakenly confuse this resurgence of religion with "fundamentalism," but the two are not the same. Fundamentalism is dying. … Fundamentalisms, with their insistence on obligatory belief systems, their nostalgia for a mythical uncorrupted past, their claims to an exclusive grasp on truth, and – sometimes – their propensity for violence, are turning to be rearguard attempts to stem a more sweeping tidal change.

He then refers to a "third quality", an "unforeseen mutation in the nature of religiousness". This mutation is the move to a horizontal transcendence, or the turn to the immanent.

Post-theistic ways of understanding God

It seems as if the theistic concepts for understanding God are increasingly being questioned. Instead, post-theistic ways of understanding God are emerging. The emphasis shifts to the immanent and concepts such as pantheism and panentheism seem to capture the imagination.

What makes the landscape even more complex is what Berger (2003) calls the reality of a unified world. He refers to the permeable boundaries between the natural and supernatural world; between human beings and the spirit world; between human beings and animals. It is a mythic reality in which humans experience themselves as being part of the cosmic whole. This is a worldview where the "mythic matrix" is very much part of reality. Berger (2003) says:

> It would be a mistake to see this worldview as being left behind once and for all. It is curiously replicated in the development of children – every child lives in a mythic world before being socialised into what we now consider reality – and it also resurfaces in certain forms of psychosis. But it is also available to adults with perfectly respectable psychiatric profiles. Throughout history, in all cultures, the mythic matrix has again and again reasserted itself, typically to the great annoyance of the guardians of the official definitions of reality...

> Its attractiveness lies, precisely, in the aforementioned perception of human existence as part of a sheltering cosmic harmony, in which all tensions and contradictions are resolved.

It is within this complex and even paradoxical landscape of movements and counter-movements that the conversation about the rationality of faith is taking place.

Conclusion

Keeping all this in mind, I would come to the preliminary conclusion that Christians today are looking for language through which they can express their faith in rational categories, but there also seems to be an uneasiness with a purely rationalistic approach to faith. Therefore the language that is used for the formulation of faith concepts should speak of rational reasoning, but at the same time be mindful of the mythic matrix (Berger) which is also part of the faith landscape.

There is clearly a big difference in the way that religious concepts are formulated in different communities in the world and in South Africa. The communities that are more influenced by a scientifically-informed worldview and by Western philosophy are probably more concerned with the intellectually plausible formulation of faith concepts. But even there one would find a strong sentiment against a rationalistic approach. Christians would perhaps be sceptical of traditional doctrinal concepts that no longer make any sense to them, but they would at the same time be very sceptical of the negative and rationalistic approach to religion as, for instance, found in the works of Richard Dawkins. A remark by Grayling (2014:3) where he, in an arrogant way, refers to "more advanced and educated societies" is an example of such a narrow understanding of reality, which does not include the value and truth of different worldviews and the value of a diversity of cultural experiences.

Thus, the mix between a rational understanding and formulation of the faith, on the one hand, and the mythical embeddedness of those spiritual concepts, on the other, is not the same in all contexts. But the reality is that believers tend to include different and even paradoxical ideas into their religious and spiritual frame of mind. In some cases there would be a stronger emphasis on the intellectually plausible formulation of the faith, but in all cases there would probably be a need for some kind of rationality. A reasonable explanation for spiritual experiences is sometimes pushed further away, but somewhere along the line people are confronted with the need to find an explanation for things. How that explanation is formulated depends on the mix of paradigms in their worldview.

The new understanding of cultures as dynamic "flows" instead of fixed entities is also applicable here. Henk van den Heuvel (2008:14) formulates it accurately as follows:

> Thoughts are developed as "processes of the mind" and externalised, i.e. made known publicly in some way. An idea or a concept is launched and distributed to individuals and groups. Again, others pick it up and they may make something different out of it, or combine it with existing ideas, thus altering or adding (new) meanings. A flow is constantly moving. It expands, every time taking different shapes.

The movement to find rationality in faith is a reality and it is growing. It differs from community to community, and it is changing in this "constant flow" of ideas in different parts of the world. Believers are looking for a complex of symbols (language) through which they can express the mysterious experience of the presence of God in such a way that it makes reasonable sense within their cultural narrative.

Bibliography

Berger, P 2003. Questions of faith: a skeptical affirmation of Christianity, http://www.amazon.com/Questions-Faith-Skeptical-Affirmation-Christianity/dp/1405108487 (accessed 20 March 2014).

Berger, PL & Zijderveld, AC 2010. In praise of doubt: How to have convictions without becoming a fanatic, http://www.amazon.com/ (accessed 20 March 2014).

Cox, H 2010. The future of faith, http://www.amazon.com/Future-Faith-Harvey-Cox/dp/0061755532 (accessed 20 March 2014).

Grayling, AC 2014. *The God argument: The case against religion and for humanism*. London: Bloomsbury Publishing.

Kearney, R 2011. *Anatheism: Returning to God after God*. Columbia University Press, New York:

Van den Heuvel, H 2008. *Between optimism and opportunism: Deconstructing "African Management" Discourse in South Africa*. Amsterdam: VU University.

Julian Müller *is Professor Emeritus in the field of Practical Theology at the University of Pretoria. After retirement he was appointed as Senior Research Fellow at the Centre for the Advancement of Scholarship, University of Pretoria.*

7

A MOVEMENT SEEKING TO EMBODY SUPPORT OF PATRIARCHAL STRUCTURES AND PATTERNS IN CHURCH AND SOCIETY

Gretha Wiid's Worthy Women movement

Lilly Nortjé-Meyer

Introduction[1]

Gretha Wiid's Worthy Women movement is the female counterpart of the Mighty Men movement driven by Angus Buchan (cf. Jackson 2009). They form part of worldwide movements that aim to enforce Christian values in family life and encourage families to live according to morals and values grounded in biblical principles. The Promise Keepers, for example, is a Christian men's movement that originated in the USA in 1990. It has grown tremendously and is an umbrella organisation for other groups such as the Christian Coalition, Focus on the Family, Christian Family Movement and the 700 Club.

I would call the Worthy Women movement a deform movement, because its vision is to encourage people to go back to basic biblical principles to restore "order" in South Africa, and this can only be done, they believe, if order in the family is restored, which implies that women should know their place as subservient wives. Unfortunately these "basic biblical principles" are interpreted from a fundamentalist, patriarchal point of view. This restoration of family order can, in turn, only take place when the man, as husband, father and master, takes *back* his rightful place as the head of the family and as the representative of Christ (cf. Buchan et al. 2006:167).

---

1 A more detailed discussion of Wiid's rationale and biblical hermeneutics can be found in Nortjé-Meyer (2011).

It seems that the desire to restore order in the country stems from the insecurity of white people caused by high levels of crime (especially violent crime) and the general immorality that is reflected by mismanagement, corruption and the spread of HIV and AIDS. A good example is Buchan's view that Africa is still the "Dark Continent" (cf. Buchan et al. 2006:158). A subtext in their discourse is definitely the problem they have with the liberation movements, whether defined by politics or gender, and the fact that Afrikaner nationalism has not disappeared (Nadar 2009b:7; Wiid 2009c; Nadar & Potgieter 2010:147). Therefore it seems that Buchan and Wiid blame the disorder in the country indirectly on the liberation of women and, accordingly, their positions in private and public spaces.

This is evident in Wiid's public discourse and her youth literature, which echo ideologies supportive of supremacy, or heteropatriarchy as institutional power, and are backed by religious control. To achieve her vision, she organises Worthy Woman conferences and focuses on prenuptial and marriage counselling seminars.[2] Although she and her husband are the architects of the movement, church youth groups and women's action groups invite her as a speaker, e.g. her Worthy Women conferences were hosted by Moreleta Dutch Reformed Church. Her conferences and seminars are well attended; around 7,000 women attend the Worthy Women Conferences each time; she appears on programmes on KykNet; her books are advertised and sold by Leserskring; and she participates in radio talks and interviews (cf. Nortjé-Meyer 2011:2). As a result of her and her husband's extra-marital affairs and use of pornography in the past, Wiid focuses especially on the sexual relationship between husband and wife (Wiid 2009c). In addressing sexual relationships, she does not refer to or define sex as recreational. Nor does she acknowledge any other important sex-related issues such as infertility, impotence, sex and people with disabilities, and so forth – all issues to which sex and marriage therapists or counsellors would normally pay attention. For this reason, Craig believes that Wiid and her husband are practising a form of emotional manipulation (cf. Swart-Walters 2010b:18–19; Craig & Stander 2009).

---

2   See www.grethawiid.co.za; Wiid's most recent CDs/DVDs may be found on her website.

The movements managed by Wiid and Buchan are not unique. They form part of worldwide movements that aim to enforce Christian values[3] in family life and encourage families to live according to morals and values grounded in biblical principles.[4] The Promise Keepers is a Christian men's movement that originated in the USA in 1990. It has grown tremendously and is an umbrella organisation for other groups such as the Christian Coalition, Focus on the Family, Christian Family Movement and the 700 Club. It claims to reach more than six million men through men's conferences,[5] and promotes the view that men are biologically and essentially different from women and for this reason their "natural" leadership and headship over women is justified (cf. Guest 2012:115).

These are examples or demonstrations of movements that reflect a particular (biblical) moral vision for the transformation of the Christian community, but because of their underlying ideology these very movements or acts inspire the abuse of women in particular and undermine proper social transformation.

How do these underlying ideologies instigate the abuse of women and alternative sexualities such as lesbian, gay, bisexual, queer, intersex and transgendered identities (LGBQIT)? Gretha Wiid draws on biblical material in her views on gender relations and identity in South African church culture.[6] Her public appearances, as recorded on her official DVDs (Wiid 2009c, 2009d, 2009e), and her publications (youth literature) (Wiid 2009a, 2009b, 2009f, 2010, 2012) demonstrate how women, their relationships and especially the female body are inscribed by patriarchal

---

3   Cf. Christian Family Movement, http://www.cfm.org/aboutcfm.html (accessed 19 May 2014).

4   Cf. Focus on the Family, http://www.focusonthefamily.com/about_us.aspx (accessed 19 May 2014).

5   Cf. The Promise keepers, http://www.promisekeepers.org/about (accessed 19 May 2014).

6   Although Gretha and her husband Francois Wiid advertise themselves as marriage consultants, she is not qualified as a minister, marriage or sex therapist, advisor or consultant. She actually describes herself as a finesse expert (2009e). She earns income from holding conferences and especially school talks and camps on sex counselling. Wiid admits that she has no professional qualifications (cf. Swart-Walters 2010b:18–19).

culture through heteronormative readings of biblical discourse and formenism.[7] Furthermore, Wiid"s public discourse and her youth literature echo ideologies supportive of supremacy, or heteropatriarchy as institutional power and are backed by religious control (cf. Hawthorne 2007:2). Therefore, she motivates her statements through biblical discourse and promotes a heteropatriarchal ideology in the process (cf. Nortjé-Meyer 2010:143).

Most ideologies of oppression work in the same way, in that they create two different categories or binaries and then assign certain traits to one group over and against the other. In doing so, this ideology places a higher value on the individuals belonging to one group, while deeming everyone else to possess traits that are inferior. Such a value system ranks "male" higher than "female", and is often complicit in ranking whites above people of other races, the upper class above the working class, adults above children, humans above animals, and so on (cf. Jackson 2003:70–71). Wiid's position is premised on a reductive binary opposition, and the notion that a man is valued higher than a woman. Although Wiid clearly declares that a husband is not the "boss" of his wife, she maintains that he is the head of the wife, as Christ is the head of the Christian community (cf. Eph 5:23–24), and therefore has supremacy over his wife. Angus Buchan asserts the same hierarchy between men and women, but also values enlightened European beliefs over "Darkest African" non-belief (cf. Buchan, Greenough & Waldeck 2006:158). Wiid applies these principles to biblical discourse to support her statements, and also promotes the inherent superiority of men over women, therefore promoting "formenism" and a heteropatriarchal ideology in the Christian life in the process (cf. Nortjé-Meyer 2005:732–734).

To be able to problematise heteropatriarchal ideology, a critique of heteronormativity is essential. This critique has two key elements in terms of social structures. The first problematises the normative and essential status of heterosexuals, which renders alternative sexualities as "other" and "marginal". The second aspect of the critique is directed at what

---

7 "Formenism" is sustained by women for, or on behalf of, men and, as with masculinism, subscribes to the inherent superiority of men over women (cf. Nadar & Potgieter 2010:141ff.)

can be called "hetero-patriarchy" or "hetero-oppression". This refers to a system of systematic male dominance and superiority. A critique of heteropatriarchy should then pay attention to its use of gender in terms of its divisions and hierarchy. Compulsory heterosexuality enforces the male-female binary as essential and keeps women *in* (within its gender and sexual confines) and *down*, namely subordinate (cf. Nortje-Meyer 2010:144). Therefore, in order to undermine this male-female binary, heteronormativity needs to be problematised.

Institutionalised heteropatriarchy and heteronormativity as social totalities refer to the systematic and systemic power and control men have over women. Therefore, in a patriarchal society, all women are continuously aware of the existence of this power against them and are affected by it. In such a society all acts of violence against women are beneficial to all men and strengthen their power over all women (cf. People's Global Action Conference 2008).

Wiid promotes Formenism

It is in the context of heteropatriarchy, and its affiliated concepts of masculinism, formenism, heterocentricity, heterosensibilities and the heterosexual imaginary (cf. Nielsen, Walden & Kunkel 2000:284) that we have to decide whether to restore the masculinism that Wiid and Buchan suggest, or instead promote masculinity, as Nadar (2009a:549-559) suggests.

Masculinism stresses the natural and inherent superiority of men and is used to justify the oppression and subjugation of women. It is the antithesis of feminism. There are three ways of maintaining this masculine power over women: brute force (physical violence), relational and positional power (e.g. belief systems) and discourses of power (everyday language, which maintains male dominance over women) (cf. Whitehead & Barrett 2001:17). Formenism is sustained by women for, or on behalf of, men and, as with masculinism, it subscribes to the inherent superiority of men over women (cf. Nadar & Potgieter 2010:141f). Masculinity, on the other hand, opposes masculinism and formenism and helps to deconstruct male power. It is a study of understanding the ways in which male power is created and maintained. It also assists feminist studies to overcome patriarchy and patriarchy's maintenance of masculine power over women (cf. Nadar 2009b:2-3). Indeed, in terms of Nadar's (2009b:2) remark about "the mystery of how a man is made", Wiid provides us with a recipe by telling young boys that they are godly men and kings, prophets and priests – thereby promoting patriarchal violence and "muscular" power in its broadest sense (cf. Whitehead & Barrett 2001:16, 400). This is an initiation into a group that is in every sense of the word hierarchically superior to other groups, for example, women and children, and that restores the ideology of patriarchy (Nadar 2009b:2; cf. Nortjé-Meyer 2011:6).

Nadar (2009b:5) argues that violence against women is seen mainly as the exercise of power in terms of physical violence or brute force, and that positional and discursive power have been ignored or even denied. This illustrates what was said above, namely that positional and discursive power exercised are not perceived by men as violence and are therefore seen by men as permissible and by women as tolerable. A good example of the power men have and what could happen if a woman does not submit is the instigation of fear. A farmer's wife said that her patriarchal husband had never lifted a finger against her, but she still feared that he would kill her if she disobeyed or challenged him, or even went against his will (cf. Maughan & Swingler 2013). How does it happen that this woman still fears her husband even if he does not physically abuse her? This occurs through discursive power and by demonstrating brutal violence against animals. When men physically abuse women, they often blame the woman for the violence, because she did not submit and obey, or because she was being unfaithful to him. Therefore, the man is exonerated from blame (cf. People Opposing Women Abuse 2010:15).

Conclusion

Wiid has no official training in Christian ministry or biblical interpretation and bases her analysis of the Bible on the guidance of the Holy Spirit and hearsay (unfounded information from unidentified sources). Moreover, people who differ from her or criticise her views are accused of being subject to the influence of the devil, and therefore want to oppose the truth. She accuses journalists of being subjective and argues that their reports are filtered by their own perceptions and beliefs. Accordingly, their misinterpretations of her analyses of the Bible are the result of their subjectivity and misunderstandings.[8] Because of this opposition and persecution, she claims to stand in the tradition of Jesus and the prophets.

Furthermore, her authoritative source of information and knowledge is Buchan. Wiid claims to have derived her approach to social issues from "Oom Angus", who says: "We should not be PC (politically correct) but BC (biblically correct)!" (Wiid 2009c). On occasion, her views on important social issues are actually frightening and are proof, in and of themselves, that she is neither equipped nor qualified to address public audiences concerning these issues, for example the relationship between Christianity and other religions, particularly Islam (Wiid 2009c); the issue of homosexuality or any other sexual identity and especially the reasons why some children will eventually become gay (Wiid 2009a:73-74; Wiid 2009b:21-22); or any political issues (cf. Nortjé-Meyer 2011:3-4).

She might speak on behalf of a small fundamentalist in-group, but she does not represent all Christians' views on gender relationships. The Christian community should be alert to the destructive influence she and her movement have on gender relationships in a socially, politically and historically complex South African society. Although her intention is to "restore" or "reform" family relationships, she actually "destroys" or "deforms" what has been achieved by the gender liberation movements. This throws the door wide open to the abuse of power, and specifically the abuse of women and children.

References

Buchan, A, Greenough, J & Waldeck, V 2006. *Faith like potatoes. A story of a farmer who risked everything for God*. Oxford: Monarch Books.

Craig, E & Stander, H 2009. *Die A tot Z van seks. 'n Seksuele verhouding met jou huweliksmaat soos God dit bedoel het* [The A to Z of sex. A sexual relationship with your marriage partner as God meant it to be]. Vanderbijlpark: Carpe Diem Media.

Guest, D 2012. *Beyond Feminist Biblical Studies*. Sheffield: Phoenix Press.

---

8   See http://www.huisgenoot.com/artikels/Plaaslik/Gretha-Wiid-reageer-op-julle-kommentaar (accessed 26 May 2014).

Hawthorne, S 2007. Heteropatriarchy: Globalisation, the institution of heterosexuality and lesbians. Paper presented at the International Feminist Summit, Townsville, Australia, 17-20 July.

Jackson, N 2009. *Women get their own "Mighty Men"*, viewed 24 March 2010, from http://www.news24.com/SouthAfrica/News/Women-get-own-Mighty-Men-20090716.

Jackson, S 2003. Heterosexuality, heteronormativity and gender hierarchy: Some reflections on recent debates. In: Weeks, F Holland, J. & Waites, M. (eds): *Sexualities and society: A reader*, 69-83. Cambridge Polity Press.

Maughan, K & Swingler, S 2013. *Love is War. The Modimolle Monster*. Johannesburg: Jacana Media.

Nadar, S 2009a. Palatable patriarchy and violence against Wo/men in South Africa – Angus Buchan's Mighty Men's Conference as a case study of masculinism. *Scriptura* 102(3), 549-559.

Nadar, S 2009b. *Who's afraid of the Mighty Men's conference?*, viewed 24 March 2010, from http://www.iam.org.za/index.php?option=com_content&task=view&id=256&Itemid=99.

Nadar, S & Potgieter, C 2010. Liberated through submission? The Worthy Woman's Conference as a case study of formenism. *Journal of Feminist Studies in Religion* 26(2), 141-151. http://dx.doi.org/10.2979/FSR.2010.26.2.141

Nielsen JM, Walden, G & Kunkel, CA 2000. Gendered heteronormativity: Empirical illustrations in everyday life. *The Sociological Quarterly* 41(2), 283-296. http://dx.doi.org/10.1111/j.1533-8525.2000.tb00096.x

Nortjé-Meyer, L 2005. Questioning the perfect male body: A critical reading of Ephesians 4:13. *Scriptura* 3, 731-739.

Nortjé-Meyer, L 2010. Deconstructing the heteronormative image of the early Christian household: Reconsidering gender as a key organising concept of family functioning. *Acta Patristica et Byzantina* 21(2), 141-151.

Nortjé-Meyer, L 2011. A critical analysis of Gretha Wiid's sex ideology and her biblical hermeneutics. *Verbum et Ecclesia* 32(1), Art. #472, 7 pages. http://dx.doi. org/10.4102/ve.v32i1.472.

People's Global Action Conference, 2008. Gendered heteropatriarchy and introduction text for the gender issues. Proceedings of the 5th People's Global Action Gathering, Athens, Greece, 20–27 August, viewed 16 April 2010, from http://indy.gr/library/gendered-heteropatriarchy.

People Opposing Women Abuse, 2010. *Criminal injustice: Violence against women in South Africa. Shadow report on Beijing + 15, March 2010*, prepared by POWA with the AIDS Legal Network, on behalf of the One in Nine Campaign and the Coalition for African Lesbians, viewed 16 April 2011, from http://www2.ohchr.org/english/ bodies/cedaw/docs/ngos/POWA_Others_SouthAfrica48.pdf.

Swart-Walters, L 2010. Verwoes deur 'n monster [Destroyed by a monster], *Huisgenoot*, 4 Maart 2010, 8-11.

Whitehead, SM & Barrett, FJ (eds) 2001. *The masculinities reader*. Cambridge: Polity Press.

Wiid, G 2009a. *Seks slim vir ouers en tieners. Verstaan jou tiener se lewe, lus en lyf*, [Sex wise for parents and teenagers. Understand your teenager's life, lust and body]. Vanderbijlpark: Carpe Diem Media.

Wiid, G 2009b. *Lyfslim vir seuns. Alles waaroor seuns wonder … oor seks, meisies en die dinge daaronder* [Body wise for boys. Everything boys wonder about … sex, girls and the things down there]. Vanderbijlpark: Carpe Diem Media.

Wiid, G 2009c. DVD: *Worthy Women Conference*. Centurion: Maranatha Christian Publishing, Brits Productions.

Wiid, G 2009d. DVD: *Seks in die huwelik – Jou lus, las of liefde?* [Marital sex – Your lust, burden or love?]. Centurion: Maranatha Christian Publishing, Brits Productions.

Wiid, G 2009e. DVD: *Verstaan jou man beter: Finessekenner* [Understand your husband better: Finesse expert]. Vanderbijlpark: Carpe Diem Media.

Wiid, G 2009f. *Lyfslim vir meisies. Alles waaroor meisies wonder … oor seks, seuns en die dinge daaronder* [Body wise for girls. Everything girls wonder about … sex, girls and the things down there]. Vanderbijlpark: Carpe Diem Media.

Wiid, G 2010. *Boosters & Busters vir 'n gelukkige huwelik* [Boosters & busters for a happy marriage]. Vanderbijlpark: Carpe Diem Media.

Wiid, G 2012. Onblusbare liefde [Unquenchable love]. Vanderbijlpark: Carpe Diem Media.

Lilly Nortjé-Meyer *is Associate Professor in the Department of Religion Studies at the University of Johannesburg.*

8

A MOVEMENT SEEKING APPROPRIATE FORMS OF CHRISTIAN GATHERING AND WORSHIP OTHER THAN THROUGH CONGREGATIONAL STRUCTURES

An exploration of Fresh Expressions

Ian Nell and Rudolph Grobler

Introduction[1]

The institutional Church of our day is experiencing many challenges in trying to connect to people in a culture that is characterised by post-modernism, post-denominationalism as well as a post-Christian mindset (Doornenbal 2012). The result of this is that there is always a search for new ways of expressing being the church that explore methods in which to connect with people in a fast-changing world. As it becomes clearer that the traditional church ministry is not attractive to many people anymore, the need for new ways of being church is becoming very urgent (Smit 2007:594).

In addition to this, new methods of church planting are being researched and implemented. New churches ought be planted in a specific context and not cloned from another context, according to Bishop Graham Cray (2009:xii), one of the leaders in the Fresh Expressions movement. These new communities of faith must also endeavour to stay faithful to the calling of Christ in means that could be described as counter-cultural. They need to incarnate into the dominant culture of the day, but must not conform to

---

1. This paper originated from a research assignment that Rudolph Grobler had to complete as partial fulfilment of a Master's degree in Ministerial Practice at the Faculty of Theology, Stellenbosch University.

that culture. An ever-present danger in new expressions of being church is that the church can easily become an expression of the dominant culture rather than an expression of the gospel of Jesus Christ.

Since the 1990s various church groups in different countries have more intentionally started to adapt themselves to the changing culture. These churches are dynamic, contextual and missionally-oriented. This movement within the church goes by many names, including Fresh Expressions, mission-shaped churches, emerging missional churches, emerging churches or missional churches (Doornenbal 2012:25). These different terms cannot be simply equated with one another, but they all have a specific focus on church-to-culture and thus church-to-mission.

Fresh Expressions has come to the foreground since the publication of *Mission-shaped Church*, a ground-breaking report from the Church of England (Percy 2010:317). Fresh Expressions succeeds in many ways in adapting to the cultural context of our day and to be missional. It also succeeds in planting new congregations. There is, however, also criticism of its theology and methods. It is therefore necessary to evaluate such a movement from a practical-theological viewpoint before its methods can simply be implemented in different cultural contexts such as, for example, in South Africa.

Terminology

According to the organisation's official website a *Fresh Expression* of Christian gathering and worship is "a new form of church for a fast-changing world that serves those outside the existing church, listens to people and enters their culture, makes discipleship a priority and intentionally forms Christian community" (Fresh Expressions 2012:43).

A Fresh Expression is therefore:

- Missional (it serves those outside the church);
- Contextual (it listens to people and enters their culture);
- Formational (it makes discipleship a priority); and
- Ecclesial (it forms church).

Church planting refers to the creation of new communities of the Christian faith as part of the mission of God to give expression to the *Missio Dei* in every geographical and cultural context (Cray 2009). This study is done within the field of Practical Theology and the researchers therefore approach the study as a theological discipline. Practical Theology is that branch of Christian theology that seeks to construct action-guiding theories of Christian praxis in particular social contexts (Root 2009:64). The practical theologian is acting as an interpretive guide trying to discern the God-human interaction in different areas of actions (Osmer 2008).

Research question

In the light of the introductory remarks and some terminological clarification, the research question could be formulated in the following way:

> What can one learn from Fresh Expressions as a movement seeking appropriate forms of Christian gathering and worship other than through congregational structures?

To answer the question we will first look at the basic theology and praxis of some forms of Fresh Expressions in action. The empirical input will be followed by examining the results through the lenses of New Testament ethics, specifically making use of the work of Richard Hays. The final part will devote attention to the way in which Fresh Expression might find some possible applications within so-called mainline congregations in South Africa.

Methodology

With regards to the empirical research, various qualitative data-collection techniques were used, inter alia unstructured and semi-structured individual interviews, focus groups and participatory observations. One researcher (Grobler) was part of a team from *Communitas*[2] in Stellenbosch that visited Fresh Expressions in London from 12-19 April 2013. During

2   Communitas is a network of committees of the Uniting Reformed Church in South Africa and the Synods of the Western, Southern and Eastern Cape of the Dutch Reformed Church helping congregations with capacity building by focusing on their calling and gifts. See its website at http://communitas.co.za/.

this time they visited and observed three Fresh Expressions initiatives and had interviews with their leaders. They also visited the Fresh Expressions communications team and met up with the Fresh Expressions team during their official team meeting. The empirical data were gathered during these interviews and the notes made on the basis of participatory observations were recorded during the reflections of the research team.

Field work

The group of researchers from *Communitas* visited three congregations in London that are very different from each other, but all of them can be identified as Fresh Expressions of Church.

- *Springfield Church* is located in Wallington and the minister interviewed was Will Cookson.[3]
- *Re:Generation* is located in Gidea Park and the ministers interviewed were Jamie and Ruth Poch.[4]
- *Moot* is located in central London and Ian Mobsby was the minister interviewed.[5]

The group attended church services at Springfield and Re:Generation on Sunday 14 April 2013. They also had interviews with the leaders and ministers from these congregations on the same day. With regards to Moot, they had an interview with Ian Mobsby at St. Mary Aldermary on Monday 15 April 2013.

a) The first round of reflection

The first thought arising from all three of the interviews was the emphasis the interviewees placed on relationships. For Springfield the main question in terms of their mission is, according to Cookson (2013): "How do we become a loving community?" and then he added: "When you select a team of people to plant a Fresh Expression of Church this team should consist of people who can build relationships, not people who are task-oriented." The experience of visiting Re:Generation left the group with a feeling that

---

3   See its website at http://springfieldchurch.org.uk/.
4   See its website at http://www.regenerationchurch.co.uk/.
5   See its website at http://www.moot.uk.net/tag/emerging-church/.

the people belong to a family. The researchers had the impression that the people formed a true and authentic Christian community. The method they use to disciple people is also deeply relational: each member has both a mentor and an accountability partner, and as soon as the member is ready becomes a mentor himself or herself. Ian Mobsby from Moot states it very clearly: "Mission in this context has got to be deeply relational".

These initial thoughts of the research group are supported by the literature on these kinds of emerging movements. According to Boren (2010) and McNeal (2011), many people are not so much interested in what the right set of beliefs is, but they are asking what is the right way to live. To put it in a different way: "What will work for me ... and will lead to the best possible life?" The test for the church today is not so much defining what we believe as it is *being defined* by how we live in community (Boren 2010). That is why relationships are so important. To confess God as Triune is to affirm that the eternal life of God is personal life in relationship (Migliore 2004:76). The literature suggests that people want to see the love of God in action in a real and authentic community through meaningful relationships.

b) The second round of reflection

Emerging from a second round of reflection on the interviews, three topics arose from the interviews and focus group data. This threefold structure emerged in a certain sense from the relational focus emphasised by the interviewees and can be summarised in three words: invitation, acceptance and challenge. These three words also gave some direction in answering the basic research question, namely: What can one learn from Fresh Expressions as a movement seeking appropriate forms of Christian gathering and worship other than through congregational structures? Or to put it in another way: What will an authentic, relational, Christian community look like in a consumerist, individualistic and secularised culture?

The answers that the interviews on Fresh Expressions produced are that these forms of Christian gathering and worship will be inviting, they will be accepting, and they will challenge people. In the next section we show in what ways these concepts were present and operative in the interview data, followed by a discussion on the meaning of these concepts.

An inviting movement

The leaders at Springfield stated that they want to go deeper *and* wider: deeper into Jesus and wider into the community. On their website their vision is stated as: "Wherever you are on your spiritual journey we would love to welcome you".[6] They have a form of Fresh Expression that is called "messy church". A messy church makes use of arts and crafts to include people and invite them to participate. It is especially focused on families and is called "messy" because there is no set structure in which things happen and everyone is really free to participate in the way they are comfortable.

The Springfield leaders strongly focus on being hospitable and welcoming towards everyone who shows up at messy church. The movement is having a strong impact on families that did not previously attend church. Care is taken by the leaders to steer clear of "church language and customs" that might alienate people. A messy church is really an open and inviting space for anyone to join and from there relationships start to form. Pastor Will mentioned that it is important to evolve and adapt to change. Springfield is always trying to stay inviting to the culture by listening to people and constantly creating spaces that are open to people in their specific context.

The first thing one notices when one meets with the leaders from Re:Generation is that they seem to be really happy to see you! We visited them before the start of their service and then stayed for the worship service. It became very clear that they weren't just happy to see us, but that they were genuinely happy to see everyone who passed through their doors! They did not have a mission statement put up somewhere or a set of core values painted on the walls, but through their conduct and character they communicated their values: love, acceptance, hospitality.

One of the leaders commented: "We make people feel welcome and no one is pressured to become part of the congregation or mentorship

---

6   See its website at http://springfieldchurch.org.uk/.

programme." Not only is the space they create inviting, the lives of the people beckon you to want to join them. There were many young people who passionately spoke about their relationship with God and what the church meant to them. The effect of this is that people from many different races, cultures, backgrounds and ages come to their gatherings. There is a sense of homecoming. One of their leaders, a man who struggled with drug addiction and was searching for God for a long time, knew the moment he walked into the church that he had come home. They welcomed him, did not judge him and showed him a new life with a new family.

Ian Mosby from Moot stated that the church must have fluid edges with a strong core. This means that the church should know what it believes and who it is, but it must adapt to culture and be inviting and open to people from the outside. Moot believes in creating spaces that will help people to meet God and become Christians. It is not about forcing people to change before they can become a part of the church, but rather about inviting people to experience God. They have many ways of creating these inviting and experiential spaces. They run their own cafe inside the church building where anyone can come and sit and have a drink or something to eat. Their "services" are very practical and seek to help people discover how to live.

Moot seeks to use the church building as a common ground where people from all backgrounds and religions can meet. They offer free meditations on Mondays and Wednesdays. Their meditation groups seek to open a silent space for all who wish to participate. They invite people to come and find rest there from the hustle and bustle of everyday life. Another way Moot creates inviting spaces is by something they call "Serum-spiritually injected conversation". According to Moot (Serum dialogue group 2013): "Serum is a discussion about all things spiritual. It is friendly, serious and fun. We explore questions about God in an informal, open and non-prescriptive way over a drink in the pub. An initial short thought and a question start things off, after which the conversation runs freely. The evening is rounded off with an opportunity to share insights and reflections." It is clear that Moot is very focused on reaching people who are totally alienated from Christianity and church. They invite people by creating spaces of acceptance where all are welcome. They communicate in such a way that what they say resonates with people in a consumerist culture.

Upon further reflection on these observations, one may say that many people don't feel welcome in church. People experience a great sense of awkwardness and inaccessibility (Keifert 1992:x). In many cases it is as if there are great barriers that keep people from truly feeling welcome. In addition to this, people from outside the "church culture" don't know how the church works. For example: the liturgy that is followed and the type of language that is used tend to exclude outsiders and leave people alienated from God and others. It is as if people have two bridges to cross in church life: the bridge to discipleship and the bridge to a new church culture.

The Triune God is a God of grace and inclusion that invites people into His presence to journey with Him. The mission of the church is to participate in the reconciling love of the triune God who reaches out to a fallen world through Jesus Christ in the power of the Holy Spirit (Migliore 2004:265). Hospitality plays a big role in showing strangers that you care about them and you want to welcome them into your space. Inviting also includes being church in the world and not just trying to attract the world to your building. It is a genuine way of being open to people and including them not only on Sundays, but on every day of the week.

An accepting movement

Springfield works really hard to be a loving and accepting community. They want to move out into the community and make a difference by building relationships and serving people. In order to be accepting, the leaders believe in a humble and listening posture – to God and to others. When we visited the morning service we were struck by the diversity of people. Pastor Will made a point of greeting new people and talking to them. There are no hidden agendas and no attempts to make someone a part of "your congregation", but rather to show an acceptance and posture of love towards anyone who enters into their community. To show their attitude of acceptance Springfield, as mentioned, started a "messy church" and a "cafe church". The purpose of these movements was to be open to people who previously did not feel comfortable in a traditional church worship service. They meet people "where they are" and accept them "as they are". This results in relationships being built and people's eyes become open to God's love and acceptance.

Re:Generation has a way of attracting the outcasts and "down-and-outs" of society. We met a number of people who came from a background of drug addiction. We saw dwarves at the worship service. We heard stories of transvestites coming to the church for worship. The members accept every person who comes through their doors, even though it is not always easy. One of the men who came to faith had recently lost his job and was struggling with drug addiction. Some of the leaders took him in, gave him a place to stay and food to eat. Through the acceptance and care he received he could start his path of recovery, but more than that, he could start living in a relationship with Christ.

The research group experienced the feeling of a diverse family at Re:Generation. Black and white, male and female, old and young, rich and poor all lived together as an accepting community. It is not always easy, but their choice to accept instead of judge had the effect of making the boundaries that keep people out disappear. They actively look for opportunities to engage in relationships with strangers. They invite people to join them in worship and create a space where non-Christians will also feel loved and cared for. This accepting space acts as fertile ground where the gospel can be shared and a relationship with Christ can start.

Moot seeks to engage people who have turned their backs on religion but are still looking for spirituality. In order to accept them it is necessary to build trust and make people part of a caring community. As Ian Mobsby stated: "People want to belong before they believe". In a sense this is what genuine acceptance is all about: the leaders of Moot know this is not easy, because people are sometimes very rugged and stubborn. But they also realise that these are the ones the Lord came to save! The members of Moot view acceptance in the following way: "assisting people to explore and experience Christian spirituality, being a soul friend to those in and outside of the community". These soul friendships challenge them to accept those who are different and to include those who are not Christians. Often this will even mean accepting and loving those who are hostile towards Christians and the Christian faith. For Moot it is about gaining trust through relationships

Upon further reflection on these observations one may say that many people have negative experiences with "church people". Christians are supposed to represent Christ to the world. But according to the research of Kinnaman and Lyons (2007), Christians are often perceived as hypocritical, insensitive and judgmental. Some who were part of the faith community experienced hurt or judgment. Others who were not Christians had a negative experience of "church people", which had a big influence on their experience of Christianity. In addition to negative experiences, many people feel a sense of judgment and a lack of acceptance. Although the church is called to be a loving community (to those inside and outside the church), people often feel that they are not accepted just as they are. There is a sense that you have to behave according to a certain set of rules before you can belong to the community.

A different type of acceptance is needed if the church is to be an accepting movement. This new community is a place where each one can experience true love and acceptance. The life of God is essentially self-giving love whose strength embraces vulnerability (Migliore 2004:81). The faith community should wear the marks of its Creator: grace and unconditional love and acceptance. This means that people are welcomed and loved as they are without being judged or rejected, because the compassionate love of God is stronger than sin and death (Migliore 2004:81).

A challenging movement

When we asked Springfield's leaders how they defined success, their answer was very simple: "Success is defined by faithfulness. Not faithful towards your tradition, but towards Christ. It is not about being consumerist" (Cookson 2013). For them this means following Jesus wherever He leads. They actively encourage people to make a difference in the community, to build relationships and to see where God is working. Their members do not just attend church; they strive to be church in the world. They are challenged to imitate Christ. This is what faithfulness translates into, for them: the imitation of Christ. They empower people to do this through teaching, Bible study and prayer, but more so by being out in the community serving others. One of their challenging initiatives is what they call "river ministries". River ministries actively seek to make a difference in the community and focus outwards. Springfield believes that this outward focus will bring growth, not only in terms of numbers, but in terms of faithfulness, producing true imitators of Christ.

Re:Generation welcomes everyone and accepts anyone, no one is pressured to become a member or forced into anything. But when someone does decide that they want to become a leader and participate in the path of growth that the church offers, then the challenge that they provide demands a lot of time and commitment. They genuinely want to make disciples and structure themselves to achieve this. Re:Generation has a very specific strategy for leading people on the path of growth and discipleship. When you become more involved at the church there are two relationships you enter into.

- Firstly, you receive a *mentor*. A mentor is someone who has been a Christian for a while and can guide you from their own experience. The mentorship relationship is still built on the foundation of unconditional love and acceptance, but there is also a challenge to grow and become more like Christ. Mentees are encouraged to be very open and honest towards their mentors. People can share their stories and pray together. Mentors challenge their mentees, support them and guide them to greater commitment in Christ.

- The second relationship into which someone enters is with an *accountability partner*. This is a friend with whom you can share your struggles and you can pray with. It is someone who holds you accountable for your conduct and trusts you to do the same for him/her. Part of the path of growth is then to start serving – both in the congregation and in the community. People who want to become part of the leadership of the church must first spend a few months serving somewhere in the congregation.

Moot seeks to provide spaces where people can start to face the challenge of living the Christian life. If you want to be a part of Moot you have to participate. You cannot be a passive bystander. Once someone starts to participate there are three spaces that Moot offers which help people to discover Christianity and to live the life of a disciple. The first space is what they call "exploring space", where people commit to certain aspirations. The second space is for deeper participation where people commit to certain spiritual practices and postures. The third space entails high involvement for people who want to dig deeper to become "new monastics" and desire greater mutual accountability.

There is a sense of moving deeper into true spirituality and deeper into community as people become more involved at Moot. Because Moot members see themselves as a "new monastic community", it involves a focus on ancient spiritual disciplines and practices. These are broken down into aspirations, postures and spiritual practices. The aspirations, postures and spiritual practices have the goal of promoting a "rhythm of life" that gives life and moves away from a life of sin. The aspirations include presence, acceptance, creativity, balance, accountability and hospitality. The postures that are adopted are characterised by openness, mindfulness, expectancy, wonder, gratitude, compassion and obedience. The spiritual practices that help one achieve this include prayer and meditation, mercy and justice, communal worship, learning, presence, mission and passionate living.

Reflection: One of the main reasons why people become alienated from church is that they do not really experience that the church is helping them to face the real challenges of life. In many ways faith becomes removed from the pressures of real life (Willard 2009a:34). In several cases it is as if the church lives in a "spiritual world" that is removed from real life and people come looking for answers on how to live but cannot find them. In addition to this, many churches have sold out to a consumerist mindset. As McNeal (2011:30) puts it: "Western culture commends a self-centred, consumerist approach to the abundant life." So many churches are giving people what they want (a consumer experience), but not what they need (the life-changing gospel and path of discipleship). When salvation does not also entail transformation, the true meaning of redemption is lost (Willard 2009a:34).

Men and women of Christian character and discipline should be formed within the faith community who are able to resist the lifestyle characteristic of a self-centred consumer society (Migliore 2004:271). The process of formation does not always come automatically or easily – it takes time and discipline (Willard 2009b:21). Perhaps the familiar saying puts it best: "God loves you just the way you are, but He loves you too much to leave you this way." The church will always be in interaction with the dominant culture in society. She must be accessible to the world but not contaminated by the ways of the world. Perhaps the best way of looking at it is by seeing Christians as people living out restoration *in* culture (Lyons 2010:53). There are many different ways of living out this challenge and the movement we described as part of Fresh Expressions help us to see the ways in which this can happen in different contexts.

New Testament ethical lenses

Although we undertook some reflection in the previous section, we also want to turn to New Testament ethics for another round of reflection on the movements just described. We found the work of Hays (1996) very helpful in providing heuristic lenses to focus on the normative question: What ought to be going on? – concerning these forms of Fresh Expressions (Osmer 2008:4). Hays (1996:2) writes in this regard: "Christians of all sorts ... have always deemed it essential that their ethical teachings and practices stand in continuity with Scripture."

Hays (1996:3-7) proposes a fourfold task for New Testament ethics. Firstly, there is the descriptive task, which is exegetical and is concerned with reading the text carefully; secondly, the synthetic task, which aims to place the text in a canonical context and seeks to find coherence between different texts by means of using focal images; thirdly, the hermeneutical task that entails relating the text to our situation; and lastly, the pragmatic task, which seeks to find ways in which Christian communities can live out the text. In the synthetic task Hays (1996:187-206) proposes three images that give a focus to the New Testament witness, namely community, cross and new creation. These three focal images serve as the lenses through which one can reflect on the movements in Fresh Expressions with some sound backing from the New Testament.

a)   *Community*

"The church is a countercultural community of discipleship, and this community is the primary addressee of God's imperatives" (Hays 1996:196). The New Testament is not written simply as instructions on how individuals can "get into heaven", but it focuses on God's design for forming a covenant people. God is not simply interested in individuals "on their own", but wants to transform humanity collectively. The entire trajectory of Scripture points to God calling out a people to embody His salvation and using these people to embody this salvation to the world. The church community, in its corporate life as the body of Christ, is meant to embody an alternative order that stands as a sign of God's redemptive purposes in the world (Hays 1996:196). In this sense Hays argues that "community" is not merely a pleasing concept, but it points to the social manifestation of the people of God. Everything the individual does as a member of the church should be rooted in the identity of the community.

Reflecting on the possible strengths of the movements described in Fresh Expressions concerning community, we see that all of the movements the research group visited showed a strong focus on relationships. The question would now be what the quality of these relationships is? Being relational does not necessarily mean being communal. In looking deeper at the way the relationships take shape, it does appear that there is indeed something deeper. People are not simply a number on a list, but are connected with someone in the community and so become a part of that community. Friends invite other friends and networks of relationships come into existence.

Reflecting on possible threats to the community experience, they may be what Beck (2002:11) sees as a form of 'institutionalised individualism" so prevalent in Western societies. This means that individuals are confronted on many levels with the following challenge: you may and you must lead your own independent life, outside the old bonds of family, tribe, religion, origin and class; and you must do this within the new guidelines and rules which the state, the job market, the bureaucracy etc. lay down. This individualism ultimately means that "I am myself by myself". It breaks bonds with the community and tries to seek the good of the self through the self. In other words, even though Fresh Expressions aims to create authentic community, the danger of individualism is always lurking. So it might mean that the break with traditional modes of church stems from dissatisfaction with all things organised and communal.

Therefor some scholars such as Percy (2010:327) are of the opinion that Fresh Expressions is symptomatic of contemporary culture, which has typically adopted the rhetoric of "new", "alternative" and "fresh", which in turn is rooted in increasing individualism, and the inward turn to fulfilment and personal enhancement. This can have a negative impact on the Fresh Expressions movement. They are still young as communities and at some point in the future individualism might cause the members to just once again break away from "the old, institutional ways" and start something fresh.

b)   Cross

"Jesus' death on a cross is the paradigm for faithfulness to God in the world." (Hays 1996:197). "The only table of fellowship in the Christian faith is the wooden table that morphs into a wooden cross" (McKnight, 2010:21). Love is often seen as the basic Christian command and ethic, but for Hays (1996:202) love is not sufficient, because it is not an image in itself but rather an interpretation of an image. The term love can be easily manipulated to mean whatever we want it to mean. It can also exclude some and include others.

What the New Testament means by love is embodied in the cross (Hays 1996:202). This means that the community of faith must be formed by the paradigm of the cross. Jesus' death is an act of self-giving love and the community is called upon to take up the cross and follow Him by imitating His example (Hays 1996:197). On a practical level this means that the way the Christian community must live is defined by obedience, self-giving and sacrifice – this is the essence of imitating Christ (Hays 1996:197). The church is a radical community, shaped by what Jesus did on the cross. This means that people are to be loved unconditionally and forgiven and served, because this is what Christ has done for us.

Reflecting on the possible strengths of Fresh Expressions in terms of the cross, we see that the way in which the movements focus on accepting people unconditionally without judgment and welcoming them with hospitality into communion reflects the way the cross shaped these movements. These Fresh Expressions movements show love to people, not because they act or look a certain way, but in spite of all these things. Strangers are welcomed, outcasts are included, and sinners are accepted. These are some of the practical ways the gospel is lived through love in Fresh Expressions. One thing that stood out was the way that the love of the cross was lived out towards people who will never feel at home in a "traditional" form of church. The radical message of the cross is lived out by a radical community of love.

Reflecting on possible threats to the paradigm of the cross is the ever-present reality of moralism. "The most common way that we in the Christian community have of avoiding or marginalising Jesus' death is by constructing a way of life that is safe and secure and guilt-free" (Peterson 2008:15). Moralism is a way of living that separates salvation from what Jesus has done for us on the cross. It is a focus on outward behaviour and correct conduct that tries to give us control and puts the cross on the margin. It imposes right behaviour on oneself and others (Peterson 2008:16).

The moment that the cross becomes an example of what we should do rather than a sign of what Christ has done, then any movement runs into trouble. Sometimes people respond negatively to the cross and then Christians try to sugar-coat the message of suffering and the way God brings salvation. Moralism is just one way in which people reject God's gift and try to make their own way. Peterson (2008:20) says that moralism works from the assumption of human ability and arranges life in such a way that my good behaviour will guarantee protection from punishment or disaster. In moralism there is no place for vulnerability. Although the research group was not present long enough amongst the movements they visited to assess this threat, moralism is always a danger to nullify the work on the cross.

c)   New creation

"The Church embodies the power of the resurrection in the midst of a not-yet-redeemed world" (Hays, 1996:198). "Therefore, if anyone is in Christ, the new creation has come: The old has gone, the new is here!" (2 Cor 5:17, NIV). In the present time the new creation already appears, but only proleptically; we now hang in suspension between Jesus' resurrection and his parousia (Hays 1996:198). As Christians we live in the tension between the "already" and the "not-yet". Sinners are justified before God, but sinners are also sanctified to live new lives in the present age. Disciples of Jesus have the odd capacity for experiencing simultaneous joy amidst suffering and impatience with things as they are (Hays 1996:198).

Living with a new identity in Christ, we know that the new creation is already appearing. In this image of a new creation we are challenged to live a new life, but also reminded that the old is still with us. As Paul said: "Now we see only in part." But we see more than we previously did! We live with more meaning than was possible before the cross and the resurrection. Hays (1996:198) summarises this tension: "The New Testament's eschatology creates a critical framework that pronounces judgment upon our complacency as well as upon our presumptuous despair."

Reflecting on the possible strengths, we saw that the Fresh Expressions movements do challenge people to a live different kind of life. They engage people on a level that seeks to go deeper into authentic life. Sinners are forgiven and accepted and invited into the community, but it doesn't stop there – they are also trying to discern what it means to be faithful to God in everyday life. There is not only one way of doing this, but what is important is that something purposeful should be done. Salvation is not simply about where we go when we die, but it is all about the life we live now, in Christ. "It is good to know that when I die all will be well, but is there any good news for life?" (Willard 1997:12).

The focus on spiritual disciplines in these movements embodies this commitment. One thing that stood out was the focus on prayer. Prayer is not just emphasised in services and on Sundays, but people were taught how to pray so that they can focus on God and grow in their faith. Moot especially had a focus on ancient spiritual disciplines to bring people into a rhythm of life that is in touch with God. This includes prayer, meditation, worship, learning, mission etc. The list can go on, but the point is not consuming religion like a product, but rather being transformed in the presence of God into the image of Christ.

In reflection on possible threats to the concept of new creation, the challenge of religious consumerism is prominent: "Left to its own devices, the Fresh Expressions movement may actually be deeply collusive with consumerism ... Is there not a danger of weaning a generation of spiritual consumers who are resistant to religious demands?" (Percy 2010:326-329). We must take seriously the charge that one of the effects of a consumer society is that everything becomes a potential commodity, even religion (Himes 2007:143). This then means that religion becomes just another object that I place in my shopping cart, designed to fulfil my every need. Seen this way people become focused on "what they want" from the church and the impact of the life-transforming gospel is lost in their lives. They become spiritual couch potatoes, flipping through religious channels until the most entertaining one grabs their attention.

As Himes (2007:143) notes, consumer culture is not necessarily a deformation of belief, but rather a particular way of engaging religious beliefs that divorces it from practice. This is exactly where the danger for the church comes in: when the goal of religion becomes the consumption of "religious goods", then growth in discipleship no longer takes place, because the consumption becomes a goal in itself. This fosters what Willard (2009b) calls "vampire Christians", who only want a little blood for their sins, but nothing more to do with Jesus until heaven.

The three focal images of community, cross and new creation (Hays 1996) may help us to gain some clarity, through the light radiating from the New Testament, on the movements described as part of Fresh Expressions. These images also provide the heuristic devices for discerning what the possible strengths and weaknesses of these movements are. We will conclude with some observations in this regard.

Fresh Expressions in mainline congregations in South Africa

De Roest (2008:251-271) wrote a chapter on "ecclesiologies at the margin" in the *Routledge Companion to the Christian Church*. He defines these marginal ecclesiologies in the following way: "Marginal ecclesiologies is a non-judgmental term used to describe the ecclesiologies of ecclesial communities which have arisen out of, or are located on, the margins of the mainstream (or 'traditional') churches." He goes on to show that these communities can have a remarkable influence upon their respective contexts because the edge is often a space for innovation. One of the groups he discusses is the "emerging church" to which Fresh Expressions belong.

According to De Roest (2008:261-263) the emerging church does have a number of common characteristics of which the first is that it originated mainly in Western Europe and North America and is variously described as a movement, a process or even a mindset. It points to something dynamic, flexible and creative, starting many times without central planning. This movement sees the church going out to others, breaking the boundaries and forming part of an outward drive. The hope is always for new processes of community formation with people in their own context and therefore it is dynamic, full of change and fluid. It often contains an anti-institutional sentiment with a lot of flexibility and a postmodern mentality. The movement wants to encourage belonging before believing and is heavily influenced by the *missio Dei* concept.

One can see in what ways these characteristics as described by De Roest are in line with the description of Fresh Expressions at the beginning of this contribution, namely that the movement is:

- Missional (it serves those outside the church);
- Contextual (it listens to people and enters their culture);
- Formational (it makes discipleship a priority); and
- Ecclesial (it forms church).

Fresh Expressions as part of the emerging church movement came to South Africa via the Anglican Church and several visits of Bishop Graham Cray from England. During the past three years the Dutch Reformed Church and the Uniting Reformed Church in South Africa invited Bishop Cray on more than one occasion to explain the essence of the movement and to train some church leaders through workshops. This contact led to the visit of four researchers from Communitas to Fresh Expressions in England during April 2013.

In an official agreement between Fresh Expressions and the DRC and URCSA the literature and training manuals were officially adopted and quite a number of clergy and lay people have been trained by making use of the material. At the moment it also forms part of the programme of the Seminarium located at the Faculty of Theology in Stellenbosch, which is responsible for the faith formation of the DRC and URCSA students preparing for the ministry. The way in which these efforts will develop in mainline denominations in SA remains to be seen. The fact of the matter is that there is a lot of energy for the revitalising of the church.

Conclusion

We want to end this study with a quote from Percy (2010:331), who offers some wise guidance on the road ahead: "The challenge for the church will, I suspect, lie in maintaining the extensive, utility and parochial forms of mission that go on each day, and are often unsung; yet also allowing the effervescence of new movements (usually associational in outlook, market-driven, intensive, etc.) that will continue to both challenge and feed the institution."

One of the biggest challenges that the church is facing today is the constant temptation to outsource its mission. We do have to keep in mind that it is not only fresh expressions of being the church that is to be missional, contextual, ecclesial and formational, but all forms of church are called to this. Already in 1926 the missiologist Roland Allen (2008:18) forecast the tragedy of outsourcing mission from the life of the church:

> In the beginning the Church was a missionary society: it added to its numbers mainly by the life and speech of its members attracting to it those who were outside … Today members of the church are

scattered all over the world, but they do not carry the church with them in their own persons, they were not organized, they very often do not desire the conversion of those among whom they live, the do not welcome them into the Church. The Church, as a Church, is not a missionary society enlarging its borders by multiplying local churches; so societies are formed within it to do its work for it.

Perhaps what is happening with Fresh Expressions is a form of escapism. So-called mainline churches that are struggling with their missional calling are escaping from this struggle through Fresh Expressions. In this way Fresh Expressions is becoming the "societies formed within it to do its work for it" (Allen 2008:18). On the other hand, movements such as Fresh Expressions may themselves be a form of escape: escape from tradition, oldness and the cost of day-to-day ordinary discipleship. Escape from the *others*, who are so different from us. The gospel does not allow this escapism. The gospel forms us into a community which proclaims the gospel, but also a community that bridges the gaps between our differences. There is much to learn from Fresh Expressions, but the church must always be church, whether it is fresh or traditional.

References

Allen, R 2008. *The spontaneous expansion of the church.* Cambridge, UK: Lutterworth,

Beck, U 2002. *Individualization: Institutionalized individualism and its social and political consequences.* London: SAGE.

Boren, MS 2010. *Missional Small Groups (Allelon Missional Series): Becoming a Community that Makes a Difference in the World.* Grand Rapids: Baker Books.

Cray, G 2009. *Mission-shaped Church: Church Planting and Fresh Expressions of Church in a Changing Context.* London: Church House Publishing.

De Roest, H 2008. Ecclesiologies at the margin. In: Mannion, G & Mudge, L (eds) *The Routledge Companion to the Christian Church.* New York and London: Routledge.

Doornenbal, RJA 2012. *Crossroads: An Exploration of the Emerging-Missional Conversation with a Special Focus on Missional Leadership and Its Challenges for Theological Education.* Delft: Eberon Academic.

Hays, R 1996. *Moral Vision of the New Testament: A Contemporary Introduction To New Testament Ethics.* London & New York: Bloomsbury Academic.

Himes, KR 2007. Consumerism and Christian Ethics. *Theological studies*, no. 68, 132-153.

Keifert, PR 1992. *Welcoming the stranger: A public theology of worship and evangelism.* Minneapolis: Fortress Press.

Kinnaman, D & Lyons, G 2007. *unChristian: What a New Generation Really Thinks about Christianity ... and Why It Matters.* Grand Rapids: Baker Books.

Lyons, G 2010. *The Next Christians: Seven Ways You Can Live the Gospel and Restore the World.* New York: Random House LLC.

McKnight, S 2010. *A Community Called Atonement: Living Theology.* Nashville: Abingdon Press.

McNeal, R 2011. *Missional Communities: The Rise of the Post-Congregational Church.* San Francisco: John Wiley & Sons.

Migliore, DL 2004. *Faith Seeking Understanding: An Introduction to Christian Theology.* Grand Rapids: Eerdmans.

Osmer, RR 2008. *Practical theology: An Introduction.* Grand Rapids: Eerdmans.

Percy, M., 2010. *Shaping the Church: The Promise of Implicit Theology.* Nashville: Ashgate.

Peterson, EH 2008. *Christ Plays in Ten Thousand Places: A Conversation in Spiritual Theology.* Grand Rapids: Eerdmans.

Smit, G, 2007. Paradigmaskuiwe in die huidige leierskapsdiskoers: Enkele praktiesteologiese oorwegings. *Nederduitse Geref. Teol. Tydskrif* 48, 594–603.

Willard, D 2009a. *The Spirit of the Disciplines.* London: HarperCollins.

Willard, D 2009b. *The Divine Conspiracy.* London: HarperCollins.

Ian Nell is Associate Professor in the Department of Practical Theology and Missiology, Faculty of Theology, Stellenbosch University.

Rudolph Grobler is Minister in the Dutch Reformed Congregation George-Bergsig, George.

9

A MOVEMENT SEEKING TO MEDIATE AND UNLOCK THE RICHNESS OF GOD'S MANIFOLD BLESSINGS, ESPECIALLY BUT NOT ONLY AMONGST THE URBAN POOR

Ezekiel Mathole

Introduction

Poverty is a phenomenon that is a reality for many people in cities as well as rural areas. Since it affects God's people, the disciples of Christ respond with various ministries intended to serve the poor. The prosperity gospel is one of the popular movements that seek to unlock God's blessings in conditions of deprivation . This gospel gives hope to desperate people who are struggling to survive given their meagre existence. Many people have to cope with unemployment without unemployment insurance; diseases without medical aid; and many live in informal settlements without decent housing. The list of conditions of squalor is endless. In this contribution I will reflect briefly on the movement claiming to unlock God's manifold blessings amongst the poor. I will compare the prosperity gospel with another movement, namely one that promotes good affluence through productivity and honest means as a Christian virtue. I will subject the prosperity gospel and the "good affluence" movement to ethical examination in the light of the biblical narratives and sociological factors.

The history of the movement

The non-denominational charismatic movement is one of the most significant Christian traditions that seek to mediate God's blessings. We can trace its origins to the USA amongst the independent Pentecostals that emerged from the broader Pentecostal movement. As Synan (2001:358) notes, "The roots of this movement lay deep in classical Pentecostalism and the healing crusades of the 1950s." The non-denominational charismatic movement became prominent from the 1970s and spread to other parts of the world driven by the growth of the "faith movement". Synan (2001:358) adds: "The faith message achieved a movement status in the late 1970s under the leadership of Kenneth Hagin, Kenneth Copeland, Fred Price and Charles Capps. With a distinctive theology that distinguished between the Logos Word (unchangeable Scriptures) and the Rhema Word (tongues, prophecy etc.), the faith teachers offered their followers physical healing, inner healing, freedom from demon oppression, and prosperity in response to the word of faith, which was a verbal confession of biblical phrases which the Lord was bound to honour." In South Africa the movement was introduced by people who graduated from Oral Roberts University and Rhema Bible Training Centre in Tulsa, Oklahoma. It is from within this context that the prosperity and deliverance gospel became so popular. Independent non-denominational charismatic churches have been planted mainly in cities by individuals with connections to similar movements from West Africa, including Winners Chapel, with pioneers such as David Oyadepo and Chris Oyakialoma.

The theology of the movement

One may say that the main feature of the prosperity and deliverance gospel is that it delegitimised experiences of lack. The poverty of people could no longer be considered as bliss. Accordingly, deprivation is a human condition that is not God's ideal for His people anywhere on this planet.

This movement seeks to show from Scripture that Christians are supposed to live a blessed life. In this context blessing implies commanding great financial resources, social mobility and social status. When people are blessed, they experience a life of abundance characterised by wealth and good health. The doctrine of God's manifold blessings is embedded with specific reference to God's call and promises to Abraham. The life of Abraham is used as the prime example of a person blessed by God. Abraham becomes an icon of being truly blessed in the following ways:

- A wealth of resources in terms of livestock;
- The land that he possessed;
- The wells that he owned;
- Huge household with numerous servants who also acted as his private army;
- Highly respected by kings such as Abimelech.

Abraham became prosperous by exercising faith in God. According to the prosperity gospel, it is therefore possible to be like him if we exercise faith: "The idea that God wants individuals to be successful, as opposed to socially responsible, and that faith itself is a success strategy, had its roots in nineteenth-century existentialism" (Meyers 2009:187). The argument of prosperity theology is that it is better for everyone to prosper through faith than become the object of charity. Being affluent is then a matter of knowing how to exercise your faith in order to appropriate God's promises of wealth, health and power. Thus the poor must master the principles of faith in order to fight poverty and marginalisation.

According to proponents of the prosperity gospel, Abraham's descendants became a strong and prosperous nation as the people of Israel. In our times the church may be regarded as the new people of God through faith in Jesus Christ. Church members must therefore claim their status as the spiritual successors of Abraham. Christians should be the new beneficiaries of the blessings that God bestowed on Abraham (see Gal 3:13-14). As children of God it would therefore not be proper for believers to be poor when God has promised them a successful life when they emulate Abraham's faith. God promised to bless those living faithfully according to the requirements of His just law. God made a pact with His people, mediated by Moses, in which He pledged to make people prosperous above other nations if and when they respected His laws. As it is stated in the book of Deuteronomy:

> Carefully follow the terms of this covenant, so that you may prosper in everything you do The universal principle to unlock God's blessing is for people is to comply with God's statutes as they are enumerated in the Scriptures. Inevitably in the process they will attain their goals for success that is lush with riches and other comforts (29:3 NIV)

> Walk in all the way that the LORD your God has commanded you, so that you may live and prosper and prolong your days in the land that you will possess (5:33 NIV).

Proponents of this movement also draw from the teachings of the prophets to show that God wants His people to be prosperous. They use pronouncements from Jeremiah to articulate God's dream for his people, saying; "For I know the plans I have for you", declares the LORD, "plans to prosper you and not to harm you, plans to give you hope and a future (Jer. 29:11 NIV). Schneider (2002:91) explains: "More intensely than any other group of writings in the Old Testament, the Prophets teach that, just as wealth is on balance the measure of God's blessings, so is it a measure and mirror of the soul." If people live in obedience to God they should therefore prosper. By contrast, people become deprived when they are disobedient to God's will. Indeed, prosperity is a divine inheritance for God's people. Likewise, we read in prophetic texts such as Ezekiel 36:11 (NIV): "I will increase the number of men and animals upon you, and they will be fruitful and become numerous. I will settle people on you as in the past and will make you prosper more than before. Then you will know that I am the Lord."

Proponents of the gospel of health and wealth also draw on the Gospels to indicate that Jesus was against poverty and propagated affluence. They make special reference to the account of Jesus' ministry as described in John 10:10 (NIV) which reads: "The thief comes only to steal and kill and destroy; I have come that they may have life, and have it to the full." They interpret such texts to suggest that the mission of Jesus was to make sure that His disciples are well resourced. By contrast, the devil works to increase people's misfortunes in the form of ailments, lack and death. Guthrie (2010:141) responds: "Granted, but the bright abundant living he offers comes with a shadow. Jesus' followers walk through the valley of the shadow of death before we can reach the sunlit mountains of life." It would be mistaken to think that Jesus' call to abundant life allows us to pursue our unbridled desires for wealth and comfort. Instead, Christ is calling his disciples to subordinate self-interest to His will in order to transform the world and bless others in their sufferings. Luke 9:23-25 (NIV) is relevant here: "Then he said to them all: 'If anyone would come after me, he must deny himself and take up his cross daily and follow me. For whoever wants to save his life will lose it, but whoever loses his life for me will save it. What good is it for a man to gain the whole world, and yet lose or forfeit his very self?'" Guthrie (2010:143) comments: "Now Jesus spells out the priorities for 'anyone' who would 'come after' him. They involve (1) denying yourself, (2) taking up your cross; and (3) following him. Doing just one is not an option. Two out of three isn't good enough … We must do all three: deny, take up, and follow."

Proponents of the gospel of health and wealth also highlight the portrayal of Jesus in the gospels as one who never lived in abject poverty. It is supposed that his life could have been better than that of the ordinary working people, the majority of whom were merely day labourers. As Schneider (2002:119) notes, "Day labourers depended entirely on day-to-day contracts. Often they had no real estate inheritance to fall back on, and, even if they managed to get by, they certainly had little security in their lives. They were poor by any standard." By contrast, Jesus and his family had a trade as carpenters, and he learnt that trade. In his birthplace Jesus was known as both "a carpenter's son" (Matt 13:55) and "a carpenter" himself (Mk 6:3). Schneider (2002:125) concludes on this basis: "For the greater part of his life, then, it seems Jesus worked at this trade. That is why New Testament scholars Walter Pilgrim and Martin Hengel and others judge that Jesus did not grow up in poverty but belonged to the lower middle class of His day." The conclusion is that he could ply his trade in order to earn a decent income.

Proponents of the prosperity gospel finally also draw on the letters of the apostles to substantiate their teaching. In his letter to the church in Ephesus Paul notes that God the Father has equipped believers "with every spiritual blessing in Christ" (Eph 1:3). Followers of Christ are therefore blessed in a holistic way both spiritually and materially. In his letter the apostle Peter highlights how God exercised his power to "give us everything we need for a godly life" (2 Peter 1:3). This leads to the conviction that God made provision for everything that the disciples of Jesus may require to live a good life. The interpretation of such apostolic teachings is rather stretched. The apostles themselves lived simple and modest lives as far as we can deduce from their writings. They were constantly harassed, persecuted and even incarcerated so that they would hardly find opportunities to live an ostentatious life. Paul testifies about having to learn to be "content in any and every situation, whether fed or hungry, whether living in plenty or in want" (Phil 4:12, NIV)). He lived without social and economic security for most of his life. Peter considers suffering for the gospel as a form of blessing. In 1 Peter 4:14 (NIV) we read: "If you are insulted because of the name of Christ, you are blessed, for the Spirit of glory and of God rests on you." Being blessed therefore does not mean you will not have any challenges in your journey of faith.

The teachers of the prosperity gospel

The teachers of the prosperity gospel themselves serve as models for such blessedness – which often borders on a lifestyle of sheer opulence. There is even a list of the wealthiest pastors in the world that includes individuals in Africa, the USA, Europe, Asia and South Africa. On that list a church leader's net worth is benchmarked applying the same criteria used in the corporate world to determine US$ millionaires and billionaires. These wealthy church leaders structure their ministries using business models. They are remunerated like executives of companies and receive royalties from the sales of literature, CDs and DVDs, and of liturgical products such as oil and holy water. They can therefore afford a life of luxury, quality and style when it comes to their vehicles, homes, apparel and forms of recreation. For such leaders being prosperous means to enjoy the same iconic quality of life that corporate captains and senior political figures maintain. This high-profile life is mimicked to the extent that it is now common to see VIP protection services provided for such pastors. Wells (1989:15) comments that "Worldliness, the opposite extreme, appears whenever Christians forget the rigorous demands of the gospel".

The lifestyles practised by such teachers of the prosperity gospel suggest that their ministries are centred on themselves in such a way that more resources seem to be allocated to themselves than to the ministry of the gospel.

"Good affluence" as marketplace anointing

In comparison with the prosperity gospel one may also identify another movement operating with premise that there is a form of "good" affluence which must be differentiated from "bad affluence." Good affluence is regarded as a consequence of the creativity and productivity of diligent Christians who use their ideas, talent and opportunities wisely to be profitable, using legitimate and honest means. Schneider (2002:32) comments: "The truth is that in modern market economies the main way that people acquire wealth is not taking it away from someone else, but taking part in its creation." By contrast, bad affluence is an offshoot of using unscrupulous and corrupt ways to become rich. Accordingly, the Scriptures affirm that God blesses the work of our hands (Deut 16:15). Russell and Russell (1997:41) say in this regard: "He [God] expects us to work hard, to be honest, and to be good stewards of that which he allows us to earn." Christ commends good stewardship, and therefore he requires his disciples to manage the resources placed in their trust very well.

It is a common belief that God empowers His children with the Holy Spirit to be in a position to participate profitably in the marketplace. In God's wisdom, "it is he who gives you the ability to produce wealth" (Deut 8:18, NIV). Whereas the prosperity gospel suggests that God supplies us with his abundance and favour so that we therefore become rich through faith, the position adopted by those who propagate "good affluence" is that "God provides abundantly, but we create wealth through our hands, our imagination, our ingenuity, our abilities, and our hard work. God has called us to take an active role in bring order in our world, and in so doing, to provide our own wealth and prosperity" (Wells 1989:21). People can become very competent in investing in enterprises and corporations that generate great wealth for investors. They also encourage the creation of employment opportunities and business ventures that also create revenue for the state through taxation, levies, licenses and duties.

Those anointed for the marketplace can become Christ's ambassadors as they engage in their ventures. Addressing people in the marketplace, Ed Silvoso (2002:195) states: "You are anointed for business – God's business. Your job is your pulpit, and the marketplace your parish. You have been called to bring God's kingdom to the marketplace... Go for it." Highly resourced Christians can use their resources to fund the work of the ministry. Jesus had numerous women as disciples who were helping to support his ministry out of their own means (Luke 8:3). A disciple may be very wealthy as an astute businessperson, but may still be compassionate enough to share with those who are deprived. Chilton (1990:39) comments: "Our purpose in life is not to become wealthy, but to serve God and our neighbour. God gives us power to get wealth, not exclusively for our own sakes." This gospel promoting "good affluence" purports that Christians can become rich legitimately by using their God-given gifts with a good conscience.

The ministry of deliverance

On our continent some of the teachers of the prosperity theology have adapted it and integrated it within their theology of deliverance. The deliverance movement is popular in West Africa and has been introduced by non-denominational charismatic church leaders of West-African descent who have planted churches almost everywhere in South African cities. It may be linked to the movement where it is assumed that God's people are not supposed to live in want. God wants human beings to experience a life of plenty, given the abundance of what God provides. It is therefore not right for anyone to live in poverty, because this is not the life that God intended for His children. Instead, it is a by-product of Satanic misfortunes that are contrary to God's wishes: "They see the world and human life infested with demons. At the same time, they firmly believe that their lives are in the hands of God, who acts to overcome these demonic forces" (Shaull and Cesar 2000:162). They see their ministry of deliverance as a ministry against forces of darkness that perpetuate poor people's poverty and oppression against God's will. Accordingly, we must reject with contempt deprivation as an existence perpetrated by demonic forces. As spiritual beings we are engaged in spiritual warfare against the powers of darkness that seek to steal our blessings: "While the devil was defeated on the cross, he is not yet off the scene in the lake of fire, and meanwhile he is a formidable enemy" (Wagner 1988:191).

Accordingly, drawing on Luke's gospel, Christ was empowered by God with the Spirit in His ministry to destroy all forms of oppressions that humanity experienced here on earth (Lk 4:18-19). Jesus came to fulfil the messianic promise that was foretold by the prophet Isaiah and that would be accompanied by blessings of deliverance from any possible yoke experienced by God's people (Is 61:1-2). Those propagating a deliverance ministry as part of the movement of the Spirit seek to promote the Spirit's freedom in the world by fighting all demonic forces that subjugate people to a life that is not compatible with the genuine freedom of the Holy Spirit. The authentic presence of God's Spirit amongst God's people should be characterised by liberty (2 Cor 3:17, NKJV). As Wagner (1988:128) notes, "By the same Holy Spirit we can be filled, empowered and commissioned to do the works of the Father."

The panacea against any kind of want is the ministry of deliverance from Satanic power over one's life. It is believed that people come under diabolic influence through sinful living and when a curse is placed upon our lives by wicked people or generational mishaps linked to one's ancestors. The result may be that a person experiences bad luck and misfortunes that make his or her life unfruitful and miserable. It is recommended that people who are oppressed by demonic powers should be prayed for by highly anointed ministers who have been endowed with "anointing for deliverance". Teaching and prayer for deliverance are practised on the basis of the model in the early church under Paul's leadership (2 Cor 1:10-11). Charismatic leaders seek to stir people's faith experience with the spectacular power of the Spirit, working on their behalf to free them from any misery caused by Satan. They raise people's hopes and courage to fight evil forces that are blamed for their hardships. In certain instances those who are suffering as a result of Satanic attacks are advised to take "holy water" and apply special "anointment oil". When holy water and anointment oil are applied, this is believed to release powers that break demonic powers over a person's life. It is claimed that these healing elements have been harvested and prepared under special conditions to preserve their potency to neutralise adverse demonic conditions.

Comments on the charismatic movement unlocking prosperity

There is a realisation amongst some within this movement who realise that to mediate God's blessings is rather more complex than offering simplistic and sometimes exaggerated solutions. It requires more than confession, prayer and anointing; it requires a serious structural transformation of society, social justice and partnerships between church, state and society. There are no quick fixes. What is required is the humility to face our sins of commission and omission, personally and corporately.

To mediate God's blessings a complex set of factors has to be considered, outlined below

a) The historical context: In South Africa the legacy of apartheid still lingers after 20 years of democracy. Apartheid social engineering is still evident, especially in the patterns of human settlement, which occur largely according to race and economic status. Poverty, violence, illiteracy, poor sanitation, dysfunctional institutions and unemployment are rampant in old apartheid townships, squatter camps and the former Bantustans. People living in these areas are mostly vulnerable to harsh living conditions created by accidental fires and extreme weather conditions such as incessant rains followed by flooding. They have little or no security and they tend to be just one accident away from more hardships.

b) Socio-economic factors: Samuel and Sugden (1999:341) note that "It has been stated in the Oxford Declaration of Christian Faith and Economics of January 1990 that economic power can be concentrated in the hands of a few people in a market economy. When that occurs political decisions tend to be made for economic reasons and the average member of society is politically and economically marginalized." This is evident in South Africa, where monopolies and corrupt cabals in the construction and food industries have been operating in collusion, leading to price fixing to the detriment of consumers and the economy. They have been using underhand tactics to raise the share price and market value of their so-called blue-chip stocks through bribery and kickbacks to those who manage tenders.

c) The political environment: In the current political environment people decry the ruling party for ignoring the concerns of the majority of people who are struggling. The concern is that government is very slow in addressing the basic needs of citizens and that the developmental agenda of the state has been derailed by greedy and corrupt self-serving individuals and cliques both within government and in business. Those who had been disenfranchised in the past still have aspirations for empowerment, better education, housing, and security. They support affirmative action and black economic empowerment, so that the message of prosperity and success is attractive to them.

The blessings of Abraham and Jesus in perspective

Proponents of the prosperity gospel have a tendency to interpret the Scriptures literally and in line with their immediate contexts: "Wealth and prosperity teachers are naïve interpreters of the Bible. Specifically, they treat the Bible as a collection of unrelated proof texts" (Wells 1989:105). They seek to find divine solutions for creating prosperity for those who are suffering. But these charismatic teachers of prosperity have failed to rescue the majority of the poor out of poverty. Instead, they themselves have become very rich whilst their followers have remained poor. They have increased their net worth to be dollar billionaires and live lavish lifestyles, enjoying material prosperity associated only with wealthy capitalist moguls.

In response, one may echo the comment in the gospel according to Luke that life does not consist in the abundance of a man's possession (Lk 12:15). Instead, the interests and needs of others must be put above our own in order to pursue God salvific purpose. Accordingly, Abraham's blessings mandate us to be a blessing to other families rather than to indulge in God's blessings on our own (Gen 12:3). Being blessed does not mean that one's life must be focused on enjoying material resources extravagantly.

Jesus was not a self-aggrandising protagonist, as some would portray him. The gospels clearly suggest that Jesus was pursuing God's mission as a servant. Through his life and ministry He prioritised the needs of others. He ministered to the poor, sick, broken, sinners, physically challenged, religious and wealthy alike. He redeemed others through servanthood. One may conclude that Jesus demands self-sacrifice, self-denial and servanthood from all who follow Him. According to Matthew's gospel, Jesus said that "anyone who does not take up his cross and follow me is not worthy of me. Whoever finds his life will lose it, and whoever loses his life for my sake, will find it" (Matt 10:38-39, NIV).

The priority of justice

Some proponents of the prosperity gospel are rediscovering the need to prioritise social justice. In response it has to be said that prosperity is not experienced by all. People are marginalised through unjust socio-economic and political practices to the extent that they are deprived. Meyers (2009:193) comments: "One of the convenient truths about the prosperity gospel is that it attracts people who are wealthy but want more with less guilt ... or promises a miracle to those who are in desperate straits and on the verge of financial ruin. Either way it plays with anxiety." To mediate and unlock God's manifold blessings for all we also need justice for all. God's people will not enjoy God's blessings when exploitative societal structures remain in place. Inequality, oppression and suffering will persist wherever justice does not reign.

God's manifold blessings cannot be mediated without considering people's access to good education and essential services. Access to such services empowers people. As Meyers (2009:199) notes, "What biblical justice does is to restore what is denied, whether it's freedom, human dignity, or the essentials of existence itself." Good education enables a person to acquire knowledge, skill and values that allow them to participate in society as conscientious citizens. Through decent education it becomes possible for them to be employable or even entrepreneurial and therefore to generate enough income to be self-supporting.

Good affluence

When profit becomes the driving motive, noble values are easily suppressed through greed and graft. Christians may attain wealth though legitimate means without violating biblical values, but they still have to remain vigilant against the corrupting influences of riches. In the Scriptures we are cautioned against a preoccupation with prosperity that ends in idolatry (see Matt 6:24). "Whatever becomes your ultimate concern is your god" (Meyer 2009:194). There are also biblical warnings against covetousness (Ex 20:17), corruption, bribery (Job 36:18) and hoarding (Amos 3:10).

Even where money is raised with integrity, that does not make it moral. It tends to mirror the character of the one who owns it. As Wells (1989:18) notes, "Even the abundance God provided can be used for evil." We live in a fallen world in which God's precious gifts can easily be misused and tainted through unethical transactions, driven by inordinate desires. Wells (1989:23) therefore insists: "In the midst of the evil of this present world, we need the solid foundation of a biblical perspective on wealth and poverty, justice and injustice, consumption and sharing." Affluence often initially accrues on the basis of an ethos of hard work, integrity and equity. But the accumulation of capital in conglomerates may well subvert their founding values. As a result their policies are tainted by unfair labour practices, the desecration of the environment, and deals attained through collusion and price fixing.

Conclusion

The biblical witnesses typically affirm the manifold blessings that God bestowed on his people. However, how these blessings are mediated in an unjust and sinful world poses a challenge for disciples who are subject to temptation too. Movements such as the prosperity gospel mediate God's blessings in a way that makes faith look like magic. Its teachers seem oblivious to the fact that there are socio-economic, political and historical factors that must be considered before poverty can be addressed properly. This may be contrasted with those who promote affluence through hard, smart and unashamedly ethical work. There is evidence in market economies that industriousness does create economic growth and profitability for the benefit of entrepreneurs and the broader society. However, over time unjust practices may well creep into the DNA of such enterprises. Amidst all these movements we must heed biblical warnings about the perils that accompany efforts to unlock God's blessings for the poor. There are many forces that oppose the empowerment of the poor that must be overcome through practices that are sound and realistic.

References

Chilton, David 1990. *Productive Christians in an Age of Guilt Manipulators: A Biblical Response to Ronald Sider*. Tyler: ICE.

Guthrie, Stan 2010. *All Jesus Asks: How His Questions can Teach and Transform Us*. Grand Rapids: Baker Books.

MacArthur, John 2010. *Think Biblically*. Wheaton: Crossway Books.

Meyers, R Robin 2009. *Saving Jesus From the Church*. New York: Harper Collins.

Russell, Bob & Russell, Rusty 1997. *Money: A User's Manual: Avoiding Common Traps*. Colorado Springs: Multnomah Books.

Samuel, Vinay & Sugden Chris (ed) 1999. *Mission as Transformation: A Theology of the Whole Gospel*. Carlisle: Regnum.

Schneider, JR 2002. *The Good of Affluence: Seeking God in a Culture of Wealth*. Grand Rapids: WB Eerdmans.

Shaull, R & Cesar, W 2000. *Pentecostalism and the future of the Christian Churches: Promises, Limitations and Challenges*. Grand Rapids: WB Eerdmans.

Silvoso, E 2002. *Anointed for Business: How Christians Can Use Their Influence in the Marketplace to Change the World*. Regal Books, Gospel Light Ventura.

Synan, Vinson 2001. *The Century of the Holy Spirit: 100 Years of Pentecostal Charismatic Renewal, 1901–2001*. Nashville: Thomas Nelson.

Wagner, C Peter 1992. *How to have a Healing Ministry in any Church. A Comprehensive Guide*. Ventura: Regal Books.

Wells, William W 1989. *The Agony of Affluence*. Grand Rapids: Zondervan.

Westerlund, David (ed) 2009. *Global Pentecostalism: Encounters With Other Religious Traditions*. London: Tauris.

Dr Ezekiel Mathole *is a pastor in the Grace Bible Church in Soweto.*